SPIRITUAL DANCER

Reflections of a Joyous Adventure

By

Fred Alexander Fleet

Spiritual Dancer

Fred Alexander Fleet

ISBN: 979-8-6667-7086-3

Digitally available since 2013.
First print edition 2020.

Spiritual Dancer

Dedication

When I stepped into *The City of Angels Church*, I realized this was going to be a different experience. Doctor O.C. Smith stood over the podium welcoming the patrons with a song and a message of love that reinforced my years of mystical learning and instruction. He spoke of the spiritual essence in each of us, of a loving parent, a forgiving Father; that we were not condemned to live a life of misery. If for some reason we chose to live a life of woe, then it was our habitual bad thinking which was responsible and not our angelic Father. We were misusing our own divine heritage by not choosing well.

Such a message was delivered with a little lecture and a lot of constant humor and wisdom from Dr. Smith. Every Sunday when I attended his congregation, I left feeling Joy-Filled. I joined the church that first day by simply putting my name and address on a postcard and that was all he required.

A few years later, I would introduce my future wife to his teachings. Because she was raised in a strict Catholic upbringing, I was afraid this mystical format would turn her off. Not only did she embrace Dr. Smith's teaching, we decided to take his night classes to better understand his ministry based on the works of Ernest Holmes.

In 2001, we asked Dr. Smith to marry us and at the end of the same year, he made his transition; he died. We felt (and still do) the loss of his spiritual leadership, this man of God.

This book is dedicated to my mentor, Dr. O. C. Smith. Although I sat in back of the church, I felt he was talking to me directly with every lesson and I tried to live my life according to his ministry.

Spiritual Dancer

Introduction

How to use this book

I have written this book as a philosophical approach to getting closer to God and also autobiographical. I have detailed stories, exercises and methods which I have found productive in my life. I prepared this book for the novice as well as the experienced to be accessible and challenging.

I also included some reference material such as: books, courses, CD's, and other resources, if you choose to continue your studies. No one source or material can supply all the answers. It is my idea to at least share my personal experiences and various methods that worked for me.

The Great I Am

When Moses stood on Mount Sinai, he heard the voice from the "Burning Bush" instructing him to go to Egypt and free the people from slavery. Moses asked, "Who can I tell them sent me?" The voice answered, "Simply say, I Am." The Great I Am is all there is. In the following pages I refer to "I Am" as: God, The Almighty, God-self but all titles mean the same thing.

The Dance

I have written about my personal dance, my discovery, my path leading to God. I discuss incidents that have molded my life and I share these with you. I wanted to write a book that not only discussed philosophies but also my life experiences in hopes of reinforcing the information. What I have learned in the course of my studies is that all things will not work for all people. You have to discover what works for you. You have to discover your own dance.

Spiritual Dancer

Of spirit let me begin
Of spirit is all there is

When I was ever so young, I never looked at the Bible as the absolute communication to the Father. Even though at my Sunday school lessons they tried to drill this into me, I felt I had a direct connection to God. Why the Bible? Why could I not talk to him directly?

I did. And I experienced several miracles and unexplained events in my life. However, I was not taught this wonderful task. In my own spiritual tutorage, I trained myself. When challenged I disagreed with such views as a vengeful God who would punish me if I somehow mistook or misunderstood His teachings.

At the core of my studies, I realized that praying to God was not enough. Every fiber of our being must give thanks for the life we have been given. Open up your being to wondrous energy of His eternal love and swim in it.

The beginning of peace starts with acknowledging it is yours already.

As I sit, comfortable in my surroundings, knowing peace, I try not to reflect on the world and its problems. I try to block out all the pains, ills, diseases, and place my mind in a peaceful cube without distractions. I meditate upon the wonders of this planet. With this peace, I began to write this book.

Anyone can write a simple phrase in mental solitude which would leave the stress of life outside our house, but the real world resides within. What you are concentrating on this very moment is the reality of your world.

Are you watching the news? Listening to music? Are you writing a love letter or are you consumed by the media which constantly reminds us of the worst in our world? Or, in us?

"

Spiritual Dancer

The tube populates the airwaves with unlimited strife and chaos. Each day the messengers bring forth the venom, the worst it can find. We can wallow in it or we can choose not to dwell in it. Bad news sells. Does it sell because it is all there is? Is this what you really want to see, hear, and consume your thoughts?

Ernest Holmes said if we truly understand our Godliness, we could cure the entire world with a thought. Jesus said if we had a mustard seed of faith, we could ask the mountain to move and it would respond. We must undertake the mission to find the divine in us. Our challenge is to rid our consciousness of negative influences. Formulate a choice of action which leads to the best of intentions, clear mindfulness, and absolute love of you as well as for others. The moments of spiritual reflection are not just to discipline yourself but are baby steps to your enlightened soul.

Where is that faith? With all the wonderful houses of worship why does the world still suffer? Is our God at fault? Is our lack of our own oneness with Spirit dragging us down the road of destruction? What is causing some of us down the road of destruction?

I find it is so easy to place blame or to find fault. We enjoy placing the blame on others, *even on God*. Our genetics, our family, our environment. We are determined to instill violence until it destroys us. We should instead cleanse our minds, our child-like spirit, to accept the worthiness of our divine grace.

I had to believe I am worthy to prepare my own consciousness for acceptance of God's wisdom. Like inviting friends over for dinner, I have the food, I have the tablecloth, the plates, the wine, but I must cook the food and prepare my house so when company arrives, they can share the love in my heart. All who enter my house, my mind, enter in peace. I am emulating peace from my God-self. This is what I wish to share with you; this journey on how I got to this state of mind and of being. You can too.

1.   Practice Patience

Begin in quiet meditation and prayer. Keep your mind focused on receiving. Accept it. The Universal Mind has an abundant life, abundant joy, for you but you may be closed to it. You may be mired in mental sewage called doubt, fear, or negative, emotional filth and contortions. Reside instead in your majestic castle of thought where every room is filled with riches. The tower of your castle gazes upon lands which are yet undiscovered. Your tower is bathed in heaven's light. Why then are you in the dungeon of your purgatory?

Wake up. Turn off those meandering thoughts of despair and confusion and leap into the arena of vibrant holiness. Shake off your mantle of stress, doubt, fear; toss it aside. This Universal Mind wants to give you the wonderful world to live and with it all of its abundance and joy.

The great source of power lies within us. Alan Watts writes, "You don't look out there for God, something in the sky, you look *in* you". Watts' writings reinforces that the reservoir of our magic lies within. If you discovered a monster, then you created it, you fed it, and allowed it to consume you. You chose. The divine source of your strength could help or hinder you, but it is your choice on how to use it.

How many times, even now, when I become so rooted in thought on my daily activities, do I drift into regression? How many times have I had confusion in my life? How often do I seek beyond these mere walls of illusion to clarity of thought and escape the everyday web of negativity?

We would rather satisfy ourselves and expend the energy of our minds on the Internet, glued to the latest stock report, ball game, reviewing educational material for the next job opportunity, reading science journals, or even writing, instead of listening to our inner voice. Remember the voice that we heard as a child, our true self? Listen again as a child. For there in the darkness, as the child is at complete rest, does the miracle of God happen. Without the use of your intellect, or your prejudices, or your environmental restraints, your child-self awaits you.

How much each day should you, your child-self, listen to God? Just start. You may find 2 minutes sufficient to begin. Maybe that is all you can tolerate at the beginning. The goal may be to try meditating upon God-self for 20 to 60 minutes a day. Spend this time as you wake up and before you get out of bed. Some time at night, before you sleep, read a few lines of uplifting spiritual material. If you fail in this task, do not beat yourself up. Forgive yourself, and simply begin again. Each day make a concentrated effort to focus on your good.

I decided to condition myself to think of God continually. As I get out of bed, I thank God. When I pick up the newspaper in the morning before that bowl of oatmeal, I thank God. When my wife brews us coffee, which can remove paint from a sidewalk, I thank God for her wonderful smile. Throughout the day, I decide to take time out to thank God for the magnificent day He has created and enjoy it as best I can live it.

The patience comes from knowing you will make mistakes, and it is okay. You spend several years learning principle only to re-start again and again, it is okay. You will fail, fall, slip, meander around through a spiritual vacuum, become lost, and it is okay. We are imperfect. But with patience comes growth allowing self-reflection and forgiveness in knowing our true journey in this life is to know ourselves. It takes time and a lot of patience.

2.   Practice Beyond Bitterness

Past conditioning rubs up against us and drifts into our world. Our lives are riddled with reminiscences of our decisions. The car we decided to purchase, the books we read, and the friends we made along the way. And we pattern every thought from the acceptance and limitation of our past.

A friend once told me his father discouraged him from being proud of his ability to do well in school. His achievement academically and his acceptance to the honor society at his school were downplayed. The reason was his fraternal twin sibling did not share his intellect. She struggled academically, so to establish equality among the siblings, his father encouraged him to remain silent.

Late in life, this was his permanent characteristic. His entire professional life was built on keeping his educational achievements quiet from everyone. He also never finished college because someone inferred that he did not possess the appropriate intellect for higher education. He accepted this as truth.

In my family of overachievers, my sister also a fraternal twin, was held back from advancement because my mother did not want to separate the twins in school. My other twin sister resented this and other similar treatment to such the extent that when she finished law school, she changed her name and disappeared. We have had no contact with her since and that was over forty years.

I know I could expound on several tales of bitterness from our parental or environmental training, but this serves us no purpose if it did not give us the satisfaction of becoming greater individuals. Some of my friends harbor feelings of negative self-worth and take their lack of empowerment out on others around them.

Deeply rooted this behavior matures into a false ego daily when it responses to an apparent threat. Ego pounces on the first opportunity to defend its worthiness and lashes out in anger. It does not matter what station or current relationship you occupy, just know the tongue will cut deep into you. Once this individual was denied the opportunity to express himself, he now has ample venom to share with you.

Our mind teaches us. It searches our storehouse of information and defends to protect that inner child. The child who is afraid and who was wounded in a previous battle now acts out.

Mechanical release

Instructional study of your mind begins when concentrating on what you are focusing on the most. Since parental seeds of behavior have been planted, begin to sort them out. For example, let's practice exposing those dialogues you may have heard often as a child and examine them.

"You're not as smart as your..."

A teacher once told me how intelligent my mother was and I was not. That was the same teacher my mother had as a child. My mother had graduated from high school at 16. My mother compared me to my youngest sister and felt it was better for me not to even think about college because I wasn't smart enough for it; I wasn't good enough. This seed was now planted.

Our belief systems are strong especially when seeds are planted by someone whom we consider an authority figure. I discovered through reading biographies that a lot of people suffered from inaccurate, misguided comments about their abilities. Ben Franklin submitted essays to his brother's newspaper under a different name because his brother would never publish it if he thought it was Ben's. Albert Einstein was thought to be somewhat retarded in school, because his teachers didn't think he kept up with the others. An African-American inventor Frederick M. Jones invented refrigeration despite experiencing racism and a harsh upbringing. Every science journal of the time thought Edison's light bulb would never work.

I started to examine my thoughts that were not empowering and replaced them with the ones that were. The task was not easy. It is something you have to work on every day of your life. You must isolate the damage as quickly as possible and begin focusing on how you can achieve your happiness.

Sometimes it is difficult to unravel these thoughts, because they are hiding under layers of defense mechanisms. They are lurking under your emotions and justifying intent. It is not like we have a roadmap to navigate through it.

The only person who has the strength and duty to challenge those defenses are you. They are powerful only because you have given them power. My spiritual teacher, O.C. Smith would explain to his congregation about our negative thoughts, "they were planted as seeds and now they are full grown trees."

Cutting those trees down will not be an easy chore. As you chip away at those thoughts, observe the changes taking place inside of you. Do you become as upset when things are not going your way? Does your boss make you as terrified as you were before? Does music your children play rattle your last nerve? Forge a belief in yourself and anchor your love in prayer and directive meditation.

Why do we hold onto these trees in our mind? We have been inoculated in believing it's the only way. Our friends suffer with the same ills so this must be a social normalcy.

So, how do we overcome these negative beliefs? Practice a joy-filled life. Leave behind bitter thoughts of past experiences and move into the now. A new beginning. Know God is always with you. Give way to your precious spirit, create an individual way to look inside yourself and see God staring back at you. Be one with God.

Venture inside your emotions. When viewing your own emotions, it's not a simple task. They are hidden behind your emotional wall and your ego protects you from your fears. Do not allow yourself to get tangled in the past.

The past is the past. The past is gone. Forever.

You are in the *now; here, today.* Only thought of knowing begins with the now. How do you become more loving *now*? How can you talk to your parents in a loving tone *now*? How can you forgive those who you blame for your bitterness? The key is to move on! Forgive yourself for your transgressions! You cannot move forward until you let go.

In the theory of Zen, one contends that we live in a world of illusion. We view the world as we see it through a mirror of our prejudices. If such inner voice speaks louder than our outer projection, the innovator becomes enlightened creating an existence of our own choosing. Live with the idea that your mind, your consciousness, serves *you.*

Make time for you

A daily meditation of prayer is required. I find that sometimes I become a little sloppy. I practice my daily routine, feeling good and then I don't do it for a while. I acknowledge to my ego, I have reached some degree of self-awareness. I might even discontinue the intensity of my devotion to practice.

I have great excuses. I need to take some time off to complete chores around the house. My writing calls me from the empty pages I have left untouched. I might need to call a few friends, which I have neglected for so long. I am too stressed at this moment to discipline my mind for meditation. Yes, I can come up with a million excuses.

Life begins its game. Suits need to be cleaned, beds cry for making, Toby our pet dog needs to be walked or groomed. Other immediate responsibilities like balancing my checkbook and making those long overdue phone calls to my parents that must be made this very moment.

As I think about everything that needs doing, my mind becomes fuzzier as to what my spiritual intentions are. The practice of prayer shifts to the background and meditation is all but forgotten. The benefits of stillness of mind are embroiled in the quagmire of doing.

Abraham Lincoln once said, "Anything worth having is worth working for". Wisdom is worth working for.

Open the doors to your prison; climb out into the loving arms of God who awaits you. Your pain fomented by cultural ignorance will fall away from your body like departed clothing. A lucid being will radiant from the station of peace. Maintain thoughts of love.

I have often failed to practice. In mind I have never really failed. In spirit I have never been lost or forgotten. So, I remain ever diligent to forgiving myself and returning to the discipline of prayer. I continue to monitor my growth by examining the method of my thoughts. How much time do I spend in laughter? How many days do I rise to greet the day with thankfulness? Can I continue to forgive others even when I might intellectualize their weaknesses?

In order to live, I must take the time to supply my being with unconditional thankfulness and love. Not from a wife, or a friend, but treat myself to my own praise. Self-encouragement must exist quietly, outside the space of others. Quietly, inside the space of essence, quietly, and I must praise myself often. Not from ego, but from the humanism of a loving God.

What tools do you need to eliminate non-productive thoughts? Anthony Robbins in his *Personal Power* tapes mentions you have to reach a point where the pain is so unbearable; you will do anything to avoid pain. This is how you can change your pattern. He believes we live our lives in an attempt to avoid pain and attract pleasure. Imagine extreme pain for a behavior of yours that you find challenging; this is your pain. Now, imagine collapsing and eliminating the power of that pain immediately.

For example, I wanted to lose 10 pounds before an important weightlifting competition. I wanted to make weight without relinquishing muscularity and strength.

Spiritual Dancer

As I was preparing for my rigid schedule, I envisioned my weight as 10 pounds lighter. I focused my attention on the foods that cause me to gain weight. By associating the "pain" of weight gain with these foods, I developed an acute dislike for those foods. Even when friends tried to convince me to eat a small portion of these selected foods, I actually had no desire. I thought about the disappointment in myself (my "pain") that it would cause me if I had to lift in a higher weight class. I always made the weight even though I enjoyed eating my favorite foods just a few weeks before.

When you change your mind, you change your habits. Believe that the moment you realize you are in control is the moment its power over you becomes void. You do not need to suffer or feel entrapped when you can simply create an oasis to your liking. The power is in you.

3.   Your Growth is Your Own

Do not become angry with yourself nor belittle your mind for the lack of progress in your spiritual awareness. Even as you meditate or expand your material search for learning, your progress lies only in your commitment to your personal growth. There are no final exams except the ones you give to yourself. Compare you to yourself. Evaluate your progress while keeping your mind on loving thoughts of yourself.

So many of us reflect on what our parents said to us in order to socialize our behavioral patterns. My father could be tyrant. Not because he was one, but because he was raised with the idea that he was not always worthy of the affections from his mentor. My father was berated unmercifully according to my aunt and so when he had a son, the lesson he passed on to me from his childhood was from a fractured ego. I was never good enough, smart enough or worked hard enough. In school, my mother was a great student and I was not. The lectures that ensued from my teachers about my lack of educational abilities plagued my own intellectual growth and self-image. Soon, I was playing out my parents' opinions of me in my life. I doubted my abilities even to perform the simplest of tasks.

There was an incident in the fourth grade which changed my life. My mother had been helping me with my homework but I still missed the honor roll each semester by a few points. She decided that she needed to spend time with her other children, that I would never get on the honor roll. I convinced myself that only I could determine for myself what I was capable of. It was the last semester for the year. I studied hard. I brought home my report card to my mother. I had made the honor roll without her help. I was no longer tied to my parents' image of me from that day forward.

My parents and instructors are not bad people. Sometimes, they are projecting their fears, their concepts and prejudices onto you. You do not have to accept these opinions.

Spiritual Dancer

Don Miguel Ruiz's book, *The Four Agreements,* states as one of the agreements: *Don't Take Anything Personally.*

I believe of his four agreements that this may be the hardest to truly practice.

Ruiz says, "What others say and do is a projection of their own reality, their own dream." Even if others tell you how wonderful you are, they are still reflecting how they feel about themselves.

When your mind begins to echo some of that negative energy or thought that takes away from your spiritual good, remind yourself of your good and keep loving thoughts around you. Make what you believe your daily institution. Remember God made you perfect in every way. God is perfect and you are part of God. He made you and me in His image. And His image is good.

We are not damaged goods

I use this lesson, because everyone is damaged somewhere in the psyche. We were raised in imperfect situations, but we are not designed to be imperfect. Our societies are designed to measure our existence based on being placed neatly into a social slot or label. In the process of socialization, we may or may not fit nicely into a slot. We are praised only when we fit, and discouraged when we do not.

I constantly have to re-evaluate myself, praise myself when appropriate, rather than rely on others. Be mindful of your greatness but be humble too. You are not damaged goods.

With this mental determination we could heal the world. It really starts with us. Look at the release of concerned consciousness with the United Negro Fund, The United Way and The Red Cross. These are organizations of like-minded individuals sharing their love of the world. Yet the spirit of their charters started with a small group of people (undamaged goods) willing to give.

4. Do We Express Ourselves in the Spirit of Love?

A few days ago, I asked a friend of mine if he wanted to see a play about Charles Bukowski. Bukowski was a writer we were both extremely familiar with and appreciated his literary prose. My friend was not sure if he could make it, but would give me a call. Well, he never called me.

Waiting for his call, I missed going to the play. Resentment captured my thoughts. I wanted to see the play. I felt I was robbed of that privilege. Why should I ever call this friend again? To make matters worse, when we did meet a few weeks later, he had a nonchalant attitude. He said that he delegated the task to his wife to call me and blamed her for not following up. What a betrayal of my friendship. How could someone be so cavalier in his treatment of me? Why would I call anyone a friend who betrayed me this way?

I found myself lingering on this negative thought too long. I returned to meditating upon my good. After all, it was I who invited him to the play out of friendship. It was I who could have gone to the play without him, but I chose not to go. It was my choice.

Practicing mindfulness, I forgave him. He was living at the level of his understanding and his awareness and I must live at the level of mine. In the silence of my house, with the incense burning, surrounded by my own spirit, listening to the child in me, I forgave myself and moved my consciousness away from this negativity.

The act of forgiveness binds us to God. God remains in our life as a thoughtful and forgiving parent who wants us to achieve the best in this life. He leads us to the right path, the right mind, and allows us to grow.

Spiritual Dancer

Growth is our spiritual mission here

Any growth remains a challenge, replacing worn out concepts with new and fresh ideas. It means a maturity of perceptions which languish somewhere between readiness and fear. It is easy to formulate a change in our minds, but to implement a practice of continuous effort slams us into the demon we fear the most: Change.

When I was an account manager in the security field, my duties grew as my responsibilities grew. I started out managing only 10 employees. Within eighteen years with my firm, this number went to over 100. Over the years, my style of management continued to change. My success was contingent on a mental shift in my management style and application from one situation to another.

The challenge was discovering new methods to manage my accounts which had grown into multiple locations throughout southern California. Each site had a security manager with specific duties and responsibilities. They operated independently although for the same customer.

Issues arose. At first, I tried the old ideas. I dug into the operating procedures and applied the information I was given. But to little avail. I was trying to change a new problem using an old method. The method did not suit the problem.

I withdrew from the problem and focused on quieting my own mind; I meditated upon my challenges. How could I remove myself from this problem and allow the all-powerful universe to instill me with wisdom. I was determined to find a new way of thinking, a new solution.

For several weeks, maybe even months, I walked a tightrope. The outward situation was still at hand and seemingly nothing was getting any better. However, I remained vigilant, conversing with my inner self.

Within time I revamped my method of operating naturally and without confusion to others. Procedures were implemented and results were positive. Through the entire struggle, I remained tapped into the Universal Mind and felt the presence of spiritual energy surge through my thoughts.

Spiritual Dancer

The deed is never easy, especially when the pain of failure stares into your face. However, never let the illusion of your fear zap your growth.

Over the course of this account, I doubled the revenue to my company in millions of dollars. With spiritual peace I developed several unique operating procedures which outperformed any previously. Each employee received a performance raise!

My desire and motivation were never based on monetary gains. My goal was spiritual growth. My joy was watching other staff members grow and to experience their successes. I felt content when the staff, supportive of my efforts, was rewarded. I believe I left a better workplace for the staff, and increased their knowledge to further their careers no matter where they ventured.

Daily challenges require a timeout. Stop what you are doing.

Breathe slowly, do not allow your confusion to manifest and fester as negative thoughts. Find your center, your power within, and succumb to it. Always take time out of your day for yourself. Take this time to rejuvenate yourself.

5.   Protect your Heart

Every person experiences some form of pain in his or her life. In *Psychology Today* an article was written about how families are dysfunctional by design. The premise suggests that we are raised by dysfunctional families and it is normal for everyone to experience painful memories. Get over it! Heal yourself! Forgive yourself! Move on!

Most parents do not want to hear they raised their children to be imperfect, but these are the conditions of socialization. The idea of socialization is to condition your offspring to fit in. If you do not conform, a greater pain awaits you: Isolation.

In the process of socialization, families unintentionally suppress our individual spirit. Every encounter with society brings restrictions. These conditions exist in institutions like: churches, schools, and even the language we learn.

These misguided principles are not done on purpose, but out of loving understanding on how communities are formed. The first rule of any social institution is protecting itself. A society cannot flourish in an atmosphere of individuals creating independent thoughts and efforts. The community deals a harsh blow and punishes wayward energy. So, boundaries are imposed to enforce patterns of behavior determined best for the entire populous.

While the intentions seem logical, the process robs one of its uniqueness. Without proper guidance, one never fosters the inner person or the real self which is left to deal with afflictions. So should we blame our parents?

Parents pass on the best and the worst of their thoughts to the child. It is our responsibility to plow up the weeds and to nourish our lotus mind. Keep looking inward for your true self.

We spend half our lives learning and the other half unlearning.

We have to unlearn the bad thinking patterns we have been bombarded with. Even with the best intentions, we must reach into our life and continue the journey to a better self. Each day without meandering through the garbage of negative conjectures, rise up, meditate and organize your thoughts to assist the process.

Your mind on the open sea

A sailor set out to sea to find the only island where he could be at peace. He faced many storms. His food supplies were depleting and his crew was starving, but he never gave up hope. This sailor met days of unbearable heat, days where the winds were torrential or non-existent, not allowing his small vessel to move into any direction. With no winds, he orders his tired and hungry crew to row. As they rowed, he sang to them. He sang of this tropical island. His crew captivated with his tale continued to row. Ignoring their own sickness, their own hunger, they rowed into the night and for days thereafter. The sailor never stopped singing. His beautiful voice became strained. But he kept on the singing. His crew collapsed one by one, but the sailor kept on singing. Finally, his ship reached the island of his dreams. The island was populated with sweet fruit. His crew came ashore. As they nestled under the trees their spirits refreshed from the sweet fruit, they sang to him.

Your mission is living life. When you emerge anew each day with dedicated determination, vigorous, and adventurous, be prepared to sing through your obstacles no matter what arrives.

6.   Settle for Fulfillment

Choose great thoughts in weak times. Weak and unhealthy moments will come. Choose to stand up to them with the convictions of a divine titan. When an unpredictable world breaches our space, we are attempted to reverse back to that habitual negativity. The emotional pain assumes the role of our fate. It has lied dormant in the shadow of our minds, but it did not disappear. In the course of a few moments, all the years of preparations shred our good intentions and leave us wading in the murk of depression.

One summer my wife and I, newlyweds, decided to purchase some property in my hometown. My father, a general contractor, offered to help us remodel our 100-year-old Victorian home. It would be a massive job. The house was in bad shape after several years of neglect, but we saw its potential. My wife and I believed it worthwhile and we had the emotional stamina to tackle it.

Excitement fed our imagination. My dad's price was reasonable. My wife and I still padded the budget just in case the project should experience some unforeseen complications. We pictured the house being done on time and under budget. I had some reservations, but my outer world did not reflect any of my inner conflicts and concerns. We agreed on a price, a deadline, and began the project within the summer months.

In the midst of the project, the demons of my past emerged. All those acid memories of working in the family business emerged. Frustrations broiled to a zenith when things started going awry. It got to a point where I had to shut down the remodeling for several days. What happened to my mellow attitude? Where were my teachings?

Practicing John Gray's *Men are Mars, Women are from Venus,* I retreated to my cave to think. I had a dragon stationed at the front door just in case my wife decided to enter. I was embroiled in my anger with my frustration with my father, with the way the job was being supervised and doubts as to why I was remodeling this property to begin with.

It would take me several weeks to regain my cool and even when the housing project was again underway, I harbored some scars of resentment. No one is above confusion and negative thoughts. It will happen to you no matter how many spiritual books you read or hours spent in prayer. How you deal with it is where your power resides. Sometimes the best of intentions can be met with confusion.

How did I get through this? Reconnecting with the source of my strength and allowing the peaceful existence of a loving God to enter my life. I started with my loving wife. Telling her I loved her deeply and nothing in this world could come between us. Sitting quietly in meditation and focusing on my inner knowledge. Forgiving myself first then my father for everything and washing the pain from my mind to move on. I refocused my attention not on the cause, but on a peaceful outcome. I began re-reading books on great thoughts, listening to good music, watching funny movies and taking time to forgive myself. I needed to forgive myself for allowing this situation to overtake my loving heart and then I was able to forgive my father.

In the following days, I woke every day to meditation. Concentrating on my good, despite the circumstances. I reviewed plans for completion with my wife and made every effort to concentrate on the matter at hand. I used positive words to express our remodeling project and practice patience with everyone including myself.

Why is there a need for constant practice? We are all vulnerable. A disagreement with a friend, or falsehood at work, a racial remark, a lover's scorn, any anchor which has been placed in our brains through heightened emotion can ignite a destructive thought. Without constant practice our minds grab onto any seed of thought which leads us down the road to despair, to darkness. Practice robs emotional disturbances from ruling our life. Why? It happens because we never completely squelched the thoughts in the first place. Can you ever replace or remove them?

Developing Tools for Proper Thoughts

Can anyone really develop a pragmatic approach to proper inclination of thought? The question of approach is suspect. What would be considered the prudent method of achieving heightened God-self? What's really the best approach for solving problems? I believe the tools are in the learning and studying self, yourself.

Temper your life around the need for improvement. Begin with venturing outside your comfort level and ask yourself questions. What makes you angry? What makes you depressed? When are the moments you feel most alive? What brings you the most joy? When did you feel happy today? When did you not feel happy, and why not?

The idea of questioning is to begin a process of exposing ill feelings and bringing them into the light. Kick these out of your mind and concentrate on the areas where you find the greatest joy. In the inquiring process, always end on the positive side of your questioning. Keep your inquiries to yourself and do not discuss these ideas with anyone.

Silence in practicing your personal journey reinforces your commitment to loving yourself and fortifies your resistance to be swayed. Friends and loved ones can influence your direction even when they mean well, but only you can take this journey.

Accept your answers lovingly. This is only the beginning. Enjoy yourself along the way.

There is no substitute for instruction and education. However, educational wisdom comes in many forms and not just from books. I learned a valuable lesson from working with my father and my wife on the house remodeling project. I was so embroiled in the problem with the baggage from past, younger years and with my past anger that I could not see at first where to go. I responded by painful retorts and reliving every emotional scar imagined under my dominating father. My mind was in torment, I squashed what God was trying to show me and blamed it on others.

Ernest Holmes, the great teacher, said you could never solve a problem when you *are* the problem. Focus your wonderful mind on the answer. I began to concentrate on the answer and closed my eyes to the noise of the problem. The house was completed within a shorter period of time than we anticipated and without further issues. Slowly my father faded away from the project and he was replaced with handymen who were more than eager to work to our direction and complete the task within our guidelines. There were no hard feelings and things worked out the way the Universe intended.

When I opened my heart up to a loving, spiritual Father and asked for divine wisdom, situations occurred and answers became evident. I opened my heart to God and asked for divine wisdom. Calmness came. My father reached his own conclusion without any interference from me or my wife. We parted amicably from any further work and immediately tension dissipated.

It's easy to speak of wisdom but to walk the walk takes a Herculean effort. Be easy on yourself when you step off course. Do not beat yourself up. It's normal. Simply acknowledge you lost touch with God and reconnect yourself to the source.

While your problems seem to be bullets being shot at you, respond with fair mindedness and positive affirmations. Admire each moment you can to put aside the weaker thoughts to embrace the positive ones. Through our loving ways we gain outstanding awareness of our best friend. Ourselves.

Spiritual Dancer

Penetrating through Confusion
And Chaos

Preparing your mind from the fog of daily confusion is a must. At the core of your confusion is you. Remove your doubts and fears and allow the loving presence of God to permeate your spirit. The stem of confusion will not be able to wrap around you and hold you.

In the beginning of our socialization process, we were breed for communal living. The concept of "fitting in" was an agenda of dominating our species to create and sustain a community. No human being could survive completely on its own without some intervention from elders who experimented with certain dictums and found meaningful criteria to pass on to their offspring.

From each tribe of humanity has formulated and forced upon their creed certain patterns of behavior. We could not escape this initial training. Our brain patterns were fashioned accordingly.

In my case, part of my history was growing up in a family business. When I was young, I was conditioned to believe the purpose in life was to make huge amounts of money and owning your own business. Somewhere in my intuitive mind, I began to question this belief. Where did my belief come from? It came from a loving God who guided me to step out on my own and at an early age I began to develop my own world.

While our family business continued, I often sought refuge in my room to experiment with newfound knowledge. Even though my mother forbade me to mix chemicals in my room, I created several potions for fueling small rockets. I read books I purchased by the boxloads from second-hand stores. I expanded my belief in God by reading various philosophies. Notebooks were piling up in my closets that kept detailed explanations of an explorer creating his own world not limited by the one my parents provided.

7.   Quietly Wait for Your Individual Thought

When reading the book by Swami Rama, *Living with the Himalayan Masters*, he recalls a student stays with his teacher for most of his teen and adult years. The master or teacher weaves his lessons and education around life, providing one-on-one study to ensure the student not only has the devotion, but the quality of individual instruction for his particular talents and abilities.

In our formal civilizations, we are thrust into our school systems with ample supply of mental query, and soon are returned to parents without an ounce of original thought. We are patterned after our teachers, the heroes in our school books, and prepared for the community.

As children we are reared with the expectation to take our position alongside our parents. The issues of the society become ours and thus the socialization begins. With this clutter in our minds, how can we ever tear away from our illusions, strip away our confusion, and rehearse the songs of a free mind?

Pattern your behavior from mystics who seek to lavish clarity rather than deception. In my journey, while my friends were preparing their personal space for business advancement, I decided to take a different course. I decided to live in a small apartment that I called my mental laboratory. I created an atmosphere of white light, healthy ideas and prayer. Using tools, such as breath meditation, I would close my eyes and envision my universe without chaotic problems. As I listened to the cars speeding along the street below my apartment, I felt the safety of my thoughts, clarity of my vision, and positive energy surrounding me.

I ordered meditation tapes from A.R.E. (Edgar Cayce's Association for Research and Enlightenment) to instruct my thoughts. I would listen for hours after work to affirmations such as "create in me a pure heart, oh Lord". Over and over again I would repeat this affirmation. I would fill my mind completely, thinking of creating a peace within me where no one could damage or hurt me. If God was the instrument of my peace, what force on earth could rob me of it? I would light candles or incense that I purchased from the spiritual bookstores I would visit, and listen to my tapes in peace.

When the Rodney King riots raged outside my door and burnt most of the stores in my neighborhood, I sat in the comfort of my small apartment knowing God was in this place and only God. My apartment building stood untouched by the violence.

Begin your journey with great books. Mark Twain said, "A man that does not read great books is the same as a man who cannot read". Read according to your temperament, with the assurance of positive loving thoughts to enhance your commitment to peace. Avoid knowledge at the cost of or detriment to someone else. The complexity of our lives breeds several different answers for each one of us. The only course is that you hurt no one; you cause pain to no one, including yourself.

I believe our minds have the faculties for greatness. We are embedded in the endowment of knowledge and wisdom from birth. The great mystics never belittle us because of our lack of sight, but encourage us to forever seek the path which will shape our ideas to view ourselves in God's presence as He views us. Wonderfully.

8.   Seek to Display Your Ultimate Good

Seek first the kingdom of God. Find the positive instruction to further develop your cause for love. Any teaching that sabotages your efforts for love, or your effort to love yourself, or fills your lessons with condemnation of others should be abandoned immediately. You must focus your waking thoughts with compassion and love for others and for yourself.

My studies of *Pragmatism and Other Writings* by William James led me to believe that our philosophies must serve our purpose. To surrender to a dogma for the sake of popularity or convenience without questioning is inadequate; you are merely a puppet not a believer. The art of pragmatic thought means the continuous probing to expand your sensibilities to accommodate your new knowledge.

Happiness is not blind bliss. I found some individuals who blend into the woodwork of life by choosing to put blinders on. They usually confess later of the lack of direction in their lives and are forced into a world of uncertainty. Happiness is hard work. Every school of learning places a warning on its doors. Know thyself and prepare to work hard at it. This knowledge is not given away without a concerted effort. The effort comes from your dedication to detail. Your practice of a calm, subtle, undistracted mind creates an endlessly grander life design.

Justifications of distractions are the forefathers of confusion and imminent chaos. Some distractions are happiness vampires. They rob us of our time, our health, and mainly our concentration on the goodness in our lives.

These illusions seem important. What are they really? It is our minds putting forth what should be done instead of what needs to be done. It's the negative forces that try to take you off your path.

For example, reading the news is less important than your daily meditation. Studying the stock market can distract your focus and give entitlement to the outside influences on your energies. Putting your mental priorities in order will enhance your capacity to deal with daily events.

I invest in the stock market. I enjoy looking over the balance sheets and comparing the latest stock with the current market. I salivate over the possibilities of my research reaping more than mere single digit of profits. But before I allow this madness to overtake me I remember those words of the teacher, "Be in the world, but not of it." I withdraw from the madness of the world a bit and take time to be thankful for daily blessings.

You are greater than the outside world. An artist remains more brilliant than his product that he creates because the spirit for which he has caressed the muse comes from the infinite source. Each of us is creating our existence based on the logical confines of our awareness. But what are our distractions?

If we create distractions in our world and give them power, we experience our limitations. Circumventing some time constraints of the world gives you unlimited power over your mind. Concentrate on your unique relationship to God. Rene Descartes wrote, "I think therefore I am". What do you spend most of your time thinking about? Those thoughts become your distractions if they take you away from pursuing your good.

Aren't some distractions necessary for our existence? After all, what if I didn't take care of the trash nor did the dishes? I can justify any thought I so desire. I can take any course of action with relevance to my emotional temper and deem it healthy. It is my mind, so I can mistake truth for convenience of direction.

Any course of discipline for strengthening the mind surpasses an attempt at mediocrity. Thomas Alva Edison the famous inventor challenged the existing thought of the day. With laser-like focused beliefs he could light the world using electricity. His failures only sparked his imagination. Edison profusely defended his position and would not allow any irrelevant thought to steer him off course.

History lessons are full of determined souls venturing through unchartered waters. We cheer them on. However, for ourselves we condemn our adventurous soul. We are bombarded with the same setbacks, the same environmental doubts, and the same voice inside our heads questioning our every move. We need to remember that we are perfect. It is the spirit of the Father that reigns inside of us. We are gifted because He has created us in his likeness. His brilliant thought also created that equal thought inside of us. The wonderment ever present in us does the work. Can you challenge yourself to see the perfection in you?

Ignore distractions which take your attention away from perfecting the greatest you. Imagine your world already living this idea.

Begin with a vision of perfection

In order for healing to begin, realize perfection already exist. When you create a dinner for your loved one, there is a concept in your mind of what to prepare. You have prepared the meal before and know how it should come out. You visualize the completed meal. Before one ingredient enters the pot, you can smell and taste the final product. The entire masterpiece of thought has already been completed in your mind.

As a freelance writer submitting my works, it is easy to become consumed by the constant rejections. To find the spirit to continue is a concentration on the result I want to achieve. I crawl out of that state of mind and imagine the acceptance from my work. I concentrate on the reality of being published.

Professional athletes discuss visualization or image projection before a game. In the book, *Psycho-Cybernetics,* Dr. Maxwell Maltz experimented with the notion of imagining the results of practicing basketball. There were three groups. The first group practiced every day. The second group did not practice at all. And the third group imagined they practiced, imagined correcting their missed shots and imagined they completed their shots correctly.

In the first group the players' game improved as they practiced every day. The second group of players who were not practicing their game got worse. For the third group of players who did not practice, but imagined they were practicing every day, their game improved.

The power of your mind is incredible when utilized properly. My wife and I went to a "Turning Point" seminar conducted by hypnotist Marshall Sylver. One of the exercises was for us to visualize our perfect day. We were given several minutes to write in detail what our perfect day would be.

Afterwards our instructor gave us an example what he wrote for his perfect day. At the time that he wrote this he was extremely poor. He had to search in the couch for change to buy food. So as an exercise for his own sanity he wrote down his perfect day. The description of his perfect day included his wealth and property, and even what he would eat for breakfast, his workout gym, down to the skylight in his bedroom.

He later showed us his home in Vegas. In that home he had attracted his entire dream.

My wife and I took the example to heart. So a few weeks later, we sat back and we wrote our perfect day. Our day began with walking out of our house onto the beach, working out in our gym and making a few phone calls to check on our business ventures.

My wife and I laughed a little about the exercise. We knew we could never afford a house of our dreams in California, but we decided to place our dreams in the hands of the Universal Mind.

Three years later, a friend of ours from Ohio decided to purchase some beachfront property in Panama. He thought it was such a great deal and asked us if we would be interested. In Panama? The *country* of Panama? We looked into it and purchased our beachfront property. My wife Karen retired the year after and we proceeded to build our dream house on our beachfront property.

Each morning my wife does her yoga exercises looking out at the waves while I walk along the beach before the sun becomes too hot. Most of our business we conduct using the Internet and we are retired living off our pension and our investments. Because we dreamed our perfect day, and we gave it the power of our words, it became our reality. We became what we visualized and believed.

In an interview with Cary Grant, he said he was born Archibald Leach. He was determined to become Cary Grant. He designed the character and became it. There was no difference between the actor and himself.

9.   Your Mind as an Instrument

The mind must be tamed, exercised, taught to conduct your will. Direct your thoughts toward a beneficial process. In order to focus the mind, it must be cleared. Quiet. Calm.

Continual practice can achieve the outcome of a quiet mind. For some it will take months or years. Just keep at it. I will discuss some disciplines I've encountered over the years which have worked for me.

Biofeedback is a method of immediate response. When I first became interested in the process of quieting my noisy mind, I looked into the area of biofeedback. At the time in the early 80's, the scientific community believed biofeedback could cure almost anything. By hooking your mind up to a computer-like machine which could monitor stress, you could learn from the auto-response of the computer's highs and lows, the process of lowering your stress registered in your body.

However, the biofeedback industry and products were expensive. The range of prices was in the thousands. I found a product which was less than $100. It was called GSR. The Galvanic Sensory Response unit was invented by an Italian scientist to detect stress registered on your skin. The GSR would produce a high tone for high stress and lower tone when the stress was lower. You could monitor your stress levels and practice lowering them through the audible tone.

The GSR came with a tape which lasted about 20 minutes. As you became relaxed, the tone lowered and you dialed the GSR higher into the feedback mode. It took several months of continual practice, but the effects were rewarding.

At the time I purchased the GSR, it was $35. I believe the price is around $75 today.

The idea is to practice daily to achieve the best results. After you have mastered the practice you can use any tape with soft sounds to continue. The idea is to practice daily.

I experimented with meditation and hypnosis tapes which I purchased from *Psychology Today* magazine. The entire idea was to bring down my level of stress and let my mind drift into emptiness.

Once the mind is relaxed you are open to positive suggestions. With a mind clear from distractions and clutter you improve your ability to accept new ideas and to focus on them.

Meditation method

Meditation is not prayer. To pray is an act of directing your attention to and "speaking" with God or Spirit. Meditation is quietude of thought, silence.

If you decide to meditate there are several methods. Choose the one more suited to your temperament. I started with tapes. I ordered some through science journals I was reading and through A.R.E., the organization dedicated to the works of Edgar Cayce.

Tapes are packed with instruction and explain the benefits of this discipline. The awesome result is a calming environment. The challenge will be creating time, space in your home, and discipline.

What you have to do is to establish time, which you need for study. Share with the individuals in your life your intentions and an idea of when you need the time each day. Inform them this is the time you do not want to be disturbed.

In meditation you will find numerous approaches to the practice. Over the years, I have embarked on several training methods, changed practices and incorporated methods I found more suitable for my needs. Be prepared to expand your awareness.

Personal temperament is vital to your growth. When examining nature you find each flower, plant or mammal and insect touches the earth with its own uniqueness. To encourage your education, participate in activities and adventures that suit your spirit.

Power through meditation stirs the advent of continuous mental evolution. In the Bible we learn to wait in silence for our blessings from God. Meditation allows your mind to be still. Learn to sit listening to your breath and the beat of your heart.

How does meditation work? Does it clear the mind? How do you begin to meditate?

Deciding on using an affirmation to begin your mediation is imperative. An affirmation is a statement or word you keep in your mind while practicing your meditation. Words or phrases like, "I'm at peace" or "God is in my heart", have relevance to your level of practice. Repeat over and over again. The words can vary, and changes to affirmations can be made. However, practice the affirmation for at least 90 days before moving on to a new substitute.

Breath meditation is a practice of dropping into a meditative state without any affirmation. You simply sit quietly in a room and allow your mind to focus on your breath. You can begin by counting to ten. This effort is to keep the mind from drifting. If the mind drifts, this is normal. Just return to counting.

Practicing Quiet Meditation I believe is not for the beginner, but someone who has completed several years of Directed Meditation and wants to move on to another level of practice. Quiet Meditation requires the student to sit without counting or instruction and allow the mind to reach quietude. Quiet Meditation is also prudent for the student who finds Directed Meditation to be too distracting. My wife, for example, finds instructional tapes on relaxing very distracting, and have the opposite effect. Remember, there is no right or wrong way to begin any meditation or spiritual practice.

Work up to spending at least 20 minutes daily in your meditation practice. If you have children or a spouse, roommates, try to inform them you need to have this practice time and for them to respect your time. Use 20 minutes as a guideline. You eventually want to build more time into your day or what is comfortable for you.

Try your practice in the morning before the stressors or distractions of the day begin. Be patient with yourself and your progress. Your healing practices are daily commitments. If you skip or miss a day remember to pick the practice back up without making an issue about it.

Healing is a daily routine. The quagmire of events seems to create more importance in our lives and we give them an intensity of purpose. Allow this healing routine to become a habit which will move you closer to the realization of fulfillment.

10. Creating the Habit of Love

To create a habit of love, be proactive in changing your life pattern and in avoiding negativity. Take a different view of your life and redesign it. Set aside handicaps that you've had in the past. Remember, you have the power to change your life because you have the divine spirit in you.

You must keep cultivating your spiritual education. Your brain waves respond to stimuli. Research indicates brain waves at alpha levels produce peak learning attitudes.

Medical research also indicates the healing powers of a relaxed mind ward off diseases and promote sleep and recovery powers. Stress registers everywhere in your body. The mountains of daily toxic thought weigh on you and linger in your body and create disease.

A habit of love is not in a self-centered way, but in a healthful way of self-awareness and acknowledgment. Viewing your world with a loving heart promotes your ability to deal with environmental issues.

When I was growing up, my father never really encouraged me in interests other than the family business. I developed my own interest in books. I would spend my earnings from working in the family business on books. I stacked them in my closet. My interest expanded to science, poetry, music, literature and with each paycheck I flooded my small room with chemistry sets, telescopes, art brushes, printing kits, model planes, and boxes of books.

My father saw no need for these "toys" but I did not blame him for not understanding. His world was a condition of his own understanding. Not being able to continue his education, forced to leave high school to take care of the family, his illusion of making it in his universe was hard work, through personal labor. He had built a successful business, raised four children, purchased real estate, and kept a crew of several men employed. His accomplishments and self-worth were based on intense hard labor.

To blame him is to not understand him. In his heart, he felt he was giving his family the best of his wisdom. It was his path, it just was not mine. Even though his parental advice might have had the best heartfelt intention, I had to follow my own dreams and in the absence of his encouragement, I had to encourage myself and develop my own goals. I had to follow my own heart.

I chose a world filled with my individual heart-felt passion for life. As my father developed his own self-image forged through his temperament, I would make it a habit to forge my own image through self-discovery.

Convincing ourselves we deserve to be loved and healed

We question everything about our lives as to why we do these things, but we must devote ourselves to the positive energy that we are already loved. We need to prove nothing. In our quest for understanding, allow God to enter. Look beyond the confines of limited thinking and understanding. Define for yourself the beauty of God's love that resides in you.

I pondered my own existence. I questioned my actions on issues where I messed up or where I misjudged others. It is not necessary to question every decision in my life. It's not important to define your life by mistakes or forgetfulness. In life it's your table, your feast, and life is prepared to give it all to you.

Allow the questions in your life to be dissolved. God loves you unconditionally. Someone else may point out every flaw you have and be happy to write a list to that affect. Our loving God created perfection in you and it is all He sees.

We must stop experiencing the worst in us and begin to slowly, gradually reclaim perfect images for ourselves. This is a process of eliminating the disempowering thoughts of our upbringing. Now the challenge is to filter out those perceived ideas that linger in our psychic and *dis*enable them. If those wonderful perceptions of us through the eyes of our friends, family and lover are not cloaked with embodiment of love, why harbor them? Sever them.

Spiritual Dancer

What would our possibilities be if these emotions were not our anchor?

How can we find love when others misrepresent it to us? We learn to misrepresent to ourselves. Take stock in knowing you are on the right track anytime you enter a self-enriching program. When you decide to break away from the pack, walk into a program with the idea of becoming a better you. Look life in the eyes and ask for wisdom over intelligence. You dare to turn the corner to find enlightenment awaiting your arrival.

Yes, it's a hard road to travel. You will meet many kinds of charlatans on the road, but do not give up. For as much as they are your obstacles they are also your teachers. Enhance your ideas. You must go steadfast in a forward progression not a lackluster recession.

In my own life, I took on the task of reading those precious books which enabled me to envision myself in other places on the planet. Each new book offered a new adventure. Especially, those wonderful mystic books filled with possible new ways to explore my world.

How can you make this happen?

Stop blaming. Even as I write this, I find I am harder on myself than I am on others. Why? It puzzles me but the answers always lie somewhere just beneath the surface. Maybe it's because once we are born we linger between godliness and earthliness. Somewhere in our growth pattern, our earth parents drilled out of us anything remotely divine and forced upon us their limitations, their desires, their ills, their fears of their environment. We walked away defying them, but deeply questioning our convictions. Are we just some wayward children who did not want to learn?

How easy it is when I observe my family and friends for me to see their failings. I have clear insight to where they went wrong and wandered into darkness. Yes, I have quickly formulated possible ways to make them whole and to turn their lives around. I brashly inform them of my opinions and offer great, profound advice on the subject.

Spiritual Dancer

And, uh, what about my own issues? Am I as diligent at seeing my own failings? How honest am I to myself in looking at my scars and peer into my own soul? How limited have I become to correcting myself, seeing my faults? We are quick to examine and judge others and their problems, however, maybe not as quick to dealing with our own.

To illustrate my points: one year, one of my sisters called me to discuss a business matter. She was having a difficult time with her new job. The secretary was going around her back and reporting her to my sister's boss. Matters went to worse when my sister who had organized a seminar with a PowerPoint presentation was relegated by her boss to hang up jackets for the attendees, and my sister's secretary made the presentation and conducted my sister's seminar. Because of the racial tones of this I suggested to my sister several ideas to address the situation. I felt my suggestions or advice came from several years of managerial experience, and as a big brother, but my sister balked at my ideas and told me she could handle it.

Well, I became upset. How dare she share her problem with me then shove me away when offered a solution? Was it just a need for her to vent? Why did she call me in the first place if she was not interested in what I had to say? After all, I was the older brother whose life's experiences were broad from owning businesses to 20 years in management. I should be respected for my knowledge and wisdom. It was a blow that went deep inside of me, reminding me of years of not being appreciated.

However, after some introspection, I realized I had nothing to prove and I reined in my ego. I realized my reaction was my problem and my own interpretations of the incident. No one could define for me how I felt about myself. It's not my sister's responsibility to make me feel good about my experiences or my abilities. I released my anger and moved on. I remained pure in my intention to be supportive to my sister and thankful

Spiritual Dancer

for the opportunity to communicate with my sister
whether she took my advice or not.

11. Waking Up a Conscious Mind

In our daily events, our general meditations must be to wake up our sleepy conscious mind to prepare it for happy events. It's not that our minds are lazy, but rather they are filled with clutter. Our minds absorb all kinds of information. The ones which are emotionally charged will get the attention while others remain dormant.

Our brains contain volumes of impulses which layer themselves to create an illusion of the world as we see it. What are you thinking of in this moment takes hold of your entire intellect. Sometimes it becomes difficult to filter through the clutter. Negative energy, negative thought, has such high energy that the mind grabs for those feelings first and can overrun all other thoughts.

Choosing the right conduct

To refrain from evil
Practice perfect virtue
And fully tame one's mind
Is the doctrine of the Buddha.
Gautama Buddha

Any person who has not let himself go into anger, frustration, is not human. To refrain from these emotions and to practice virtue is a challenge to anyone, whether you are pursuing a life of enlightenment, or just trying to get through the day.

There are several methods readers can choose to practice mental awareness, but for purposes here we will focus on just a few. First is recognizing and identifying the problem. This awareness begins with our understanding of our emotions. Our emotions are the fuel which guides our passions. We need them to instruct us to love better, give more, help others, be passionate about those in danger, but the dangerous signs of abusive temperament are signs of depressions, anger, hate, to name a few. Most people believe if you rid yourself of the anger then that will dissolve your negative thoughts. I disagree.

In the balance of nature, you need anger because of the emotional circuitry in our brains that wires us to current events. Without emotional attitudes, we would just be empty entities living our lives remotely tied to our genetics without any forethought. We are called to our God because we are designed to be. Even in the absence of thought, or even in denial, life will not give way just to intellect and environmental conditioning alone. Even if you extinguish anger from your mind, it does not vanish itself from you. The question is not how to rid yourself of it, but how to be a victor, not a victim, or how you use it.

In *Emotional Intelligence* by Daniel Goleman, he quotes Aristotle:

"Anyone can become angry -- that is easy. But to be angry with the right person, to the right degree, at the right time, for that right purpose, and in the right way -- this is not easy."

I submit that anger is not the problem; rather it is the unwillingness to control it. How do you deal with someone who makes you angry?

Maybe what makes us angry is the frustration we have with ourselves. Why can't we do more? Why couldn't we finish college? Make a success of our music career? Why do our children hate us? We dislike ourselves to such a degree that our anger is projected toward anything that reminds us about our own shortcomings. For example, I am an overachiever. Through the course of my life, I have undermined my own efforts and have become angry if I have not reached my desired level of accomplishments. Sometimes those levels were unreasonable, but I forged ahead anyway. In the course of striving for my own goals, I became bitter with others who I believed were not striving hard enough for theirs. Why have they not taken the time to study? Why are they so unsettled? Why are they always standing in the way of their success? Why is it that they don't have enough money to pay their bills? Why are they being so dense about something that's just so obvious?

Spiritual Dancer

It is so easy to find fault with others. However, when we look into our own bag of unwanted behavior, what we see are the traits we most dislike about ourselves. These emotional threads link us to our frustration and our anger. It manifests into our world with vengeance upon those around us. We lash out without regard for anyone. Is it possible to manage our anger? Of course. Practice patience with yourself.

Begin with the right motivation. To cure yourself of emotional hang-ups, pray for the best in your daily life. Forgive yourself. Pray for wisdom. Let your mind be swelled with hopeful thoughts for the world around you. Practice mindful patience not only for others, but for yourself. There is no society on earth that can grant holiness, only a peaceful mind which rests inside each of us.

Examine your thoughts with soulful reflection. In Akong Tulku Rinpocke's *Taming the Tiger,* he states:

"On the surface we may appear to be a good person, but it's the one underneath the mask that needs to be purified. If our minds are pure, then we really will be useful to others. However, pretending to be good, whilst remaining rotten inside, will not be much use either to ourselves or anyone else."

In practicing mindfulness guard your words. Be cautious with what you say. Your words have power. Be positive in your conversations with yourself. You are in control of your thoughts. Refuse to surrender to pettiness and anger. Be of Spirit.

12. Spiritual Evolution

We have evolved which in science is our destiny. Our humanity has tackled the challenges which usurped our forbearers. Diseases like polio, yellow fever, and small pox laid to rest under the might of our discoveries. We conquered space, penetrated the atomic cell and even developed nanotechnology that can capture photos from within our stomach walls. But have we evolved spiritually?

No longer do scientists believe that your DNA determines the outcome of your existence. Recent studies in the new field called epigenetics have conjectured that your molecules are constantly changing. Each molecule is adapting, growing, and stimulating new cellular growth. Even the once-thought idea that brain cells could not reproduce has fallen to the fact that the brain does repair itself.

Current evidence shows we are larger, taller than our grandparents, live longer than our great grandparents, and have access to better education. This is not just a United States condition, but a world phenomenon. And we are evolving at an extremely fast pace. We are achieving in 10 years what took several hundred years to master in the past.

If the research is there for mental evolution, why can we not believe in a spiritual one? In the backdrop of new age, philosophical thought, several masters emerged to discuss concepts of spirituality that were not really new but were not recognized by the institutional religions. These voices were not of religious piety, but of a spiritual awareness we stumbled over in our search for God. We heard from Ralph Waldo Emerson, Ernest Holmes, Edgar Cayce, Carlos Castaneda, Manly P. Hall, Swami Rama, Deepak Chopra, St. Francis of Assisi, and the list goes on. The exciting thing about the new teachings were that they were given to an audience in positive affirmations of betterment of self.

Not every individual who walked into this new age setting is comfortable. The philosophies are not for everyone. However, countless students were looking for different methods to express what they were feeling inside. They were evolving into something different and needed an expansive way to express themselves.

Growing up in a Baptist church, I first became disillusioned with the concept that only the preacher had a direct line to God. We had to wait on his sermons each Sunday and appreciate his wisdom. The sermons were always scripted for us sinners, never to be redeemed and the forgiveness of our souls relied at the mercy of our vengeful Father. Committing the original sin we were doomed. Even when the Father sent a messenger, we killed him, and we were again condemned to live in an abyss of fear waiting for absolution from a skyward being.

As a child I became completely disturbed by the concept of a vengeful Father. I had several questions for my mother who was organist of our church. I questioned how God, a loving Father, a forgiving Father condemned His children without regard for their souls. My mom really did not try to answer my questions. She just instructed me to listen closer to the minister's sermons. I needed a stronger idea.

To confront your own weakness is to take on a stronger idea. For me, the stronger idea came in a flash. Sitting in the back of the church I awoke to a memory of being filled with holiness. I felt as if someone was pointing me in a direction different than what I was being told.

In the following weeks, I questioned everyone about how they were approaching God. I did not argue with anyone. I was floating on some cloud. It was as if was listening to the wind and found it had music in it. I studied the Bible, not to understand it, but to feel it.

Then I had a wondrous dream. The book of life appeared to me from the sky. It was so simple. But in my haste to try to understand it all, all I remember from that dream was from the book of Proverbs: "Every prudent *man* dealt with knowledge: but a fool laid open his folly."

Spiritual Dancer

Spiritual Evolution breathes into our modern minds the will to seek out God. If we allow the message to penetrate, our spiritual egos rise to the occasion and the miracles begin to happen. As we grow in knowledge the old ways slowly erode while our new thoughts continue our education throughout our journey on earth. Spiritual Evolution fulfills its promise. We continue to experience miracles because of the Spirit which has grown and lights the way.

The reason Spirit has made itself more available to us is because some barriers have been lifted. We have better access to education, better access to other cultures, religions and beliefs, more acceptable masters to teach us.

Scientists have concluded we are genetically smarter than our grandparents, but the research hasn't determined if we are more adapting to spiritual evolution than our forbearers. I believe we are. What has been labeled in the past as *"the Gods"* today we understand them to be natural phenomena. The eclipse of the moon is no longer perceived as the omen of death, but simply when the moon passes between the earth and the sun. Science not only has explained many things, but also has forced our minds to look deeper into life for miracles.

Our faith has evolved around notions which are acceptable to the modern mind. Transformation has occurred for the soul and the body to take form. Transformation is life's new paradigm.

Transformation is a life discipline where one shifts his own consciousness. Road blocks are life's message that a better method of growth is needed. Sometime we look at problems as if they are nuisances. Let us shift our mindset to a concept they are Spirit's way of answering our prayers. Instead of looking at life as solving one problem after another, imagine it is just a way to approach a higher vibration of thought, of growth.

Even with my understanding of Spirit, I often find myself questioning my own thoughts when problems arise. I go through several thought processes to deal with new issues.

Spiritual Dancer

First step of the process is recognition. Recognition helps to verify why this situation is happening in my universe. In my personal design, I have written this challenge into my life, and then the solution is to convince myself that I am the creator to rewrite it.

Second step is procrastination. My life will be demanding some sort of resolution on my part, but sometimes I take the path of avoidance. I have realized over the years that it will not go away and resolve itself. In recognizing, I forge ahead and attack my problems. By procrastination you feed the situation and create a formidable opponent.

Third step is fact finding. In this phase, I am looking for answers by gathering all the information I can muster. With the help of Spirit's guidance, I begin to sort out what is the problem from what is the problem with me. Have I been transmitting a weakness in my own thoughts which might have created what I have to experience now?

It's important for spiritual transformations to begin looking inside for results rather than blaming outside conditions. The fact finding step is a method of consciously collecting information from the situation, but also penetrating your mind looking for your inner strength. Remembering that no matter what the circumstances are, God is with you. ALWAYS.

The fact finding stage is not a simple task. In our logical upbringing we are led to believe that limited resources of intellect can solve some of life's quandaries. We rely on our current ideas to resolve our problems. We search our present day mind for answers.

My spiritual teacher, O.C. Smith once said, "A problem can't be solved with the same mind that created it". You need a new attitude. This is where the transformation of spiritual knowledge springs forth. In the fact finding phase, curtail your investigation for answers from outer things, rather sit quietly in a comfortable chair and meditate. Begin to envision the problem already solved. Dr. O.C. Smith would say, "Let Go, Let God".

Spiritual Dancer

To understand your transformation is to believe God has never left you alone. As you continue on your spiritual journey, understand He has answered the problem for you. There will be a time where you believe it too. Convince yourself that it is the Father who does the work and the work is glorious. Sit back and await the miracle.

The last step is resolution. Problems are solved according to your level of consciousness. We are spirits vibrating at the level of our understanding. Everyone is on his or her own path. I am not on yours or you mine. The resolutions I seek are mine alone. I do not need to justify them or explain them, but give thanks for them.

Resolution is the hardest step to take. We must reach a conclusion which benefits us moving forward. Some of our belief systems are patterned after the dictums that our Spiritual Father is a punishing one. He prevents us from obtaining our higher self, so He condemns us to a life of pain. In the resolution process, you must convince yourself this is not true.

We must change our way of thinking. Spiritual resolution comes from understanding our emotional patterns. Give way to God and continue with our lives.

He may not come when you want him, but He's right on time.

This lyric is from a hymn we sang in church when I was a boy. God is omnipotent. He really doesn't need your permission to enter your life, but He would love to have your cooperation. In the spirit of lovingness, His hand guides you to do well. We must allow ourselves the absence of fear and enter the world of outstanding love. Transformations begin the moment you realize there is forever the presence of your wonderful soul which has the power to do all the work that is necessary for your existence.

Are you ready for transformation? It is already happening. It happened the moment you challenged yourself to take the steps needed to let peace and love begin with you. When situations arise, do not condemn them, embrace them; allow the light within you to shine through every day knowing you are learning more about the world and yourself. There are reasons you are given a situation. Take time to love God. Listen more and talk less. Take advantage of every opportunity to thank God and to dance within spirit. Lie down in peace and know that He who gives birth to everything has saved you from yourself.

13. Have a Sense of Humor

Developing a sense of humor becomes a mainstay in your arsenal of skills. Being able to use wit to combat depression presents a mastery of words and intellect which can only produce laughter.

My friend's father could tell jokes up to four hours without repeating a single one. While watching a football game his son sat on the couch while I listened to his dad's continuous flow of jokes throughout the game.

Each joke was told with great timing of the punch lines and everyone in the room laughed throughout the football game. His grandson was playing for Georgia Tech in the championship game. When someone said that his grandson put the team in a bad position on the field, he did not become angry; he simply remarked, "It keeps the game interesting". Georgia Tech went on to win the championship and his grandson was drafted by the New England Patriots.

Laughter is a healthy massage to our bodies. Scientists have concluded that laughing pumps endomorphs into the body and stimulates our immune system. Norman Cousins realized this when he was diagnosed with inoperative cancer. He decided to take control of his health by using what he described in his book, *Anatomy of an Illness as Perceived by the Patient: Reflections on Healing,* as the laugh-cure. He decided to laugh himself well. And it worked!

Wit is an attractive quality. How do you develop it? Listen to humorous phrases and then write them down to remind yourself. Some people make index cards of jokes and store them away. Watch comedies and other fun shows on TV, listen to records, and read authors like Ogden Nash and Mark Twain who are known for their witticism and wisecracks.

Spiritual Dancer

A Word to Husbands

For my early years, I loved listening to the recordings of Bill Cosby. Each night in my bedroom, later than curfew, I turned on my small lamp, and quietly listened to the master storyteller. Without foul language or indecent situations, Cosby could weave a hilarious story. I spent hours memorizing his family's stories and later I used it to entertain my family and friends. I gained the ability to remember jokes or crazy stories and embellish a few of my own.

In later years, when I was a manager, I would use humor to dissolve an unpleasant situation or to motivate my staff. As long as the humor was appreciated, it worked. I never made fun of anyone and tried to stay away from using humor at the sake of someone else.

Cultivating a funny bone

The easiest thing to do is to make fun of yourself. Making wisecracks about yourself, in a positive way, disarms your associates, and makes them relax around you. Keep in mind that the idea is not to overdue the bad mouthing of yourself, but just to add a little levity in the mix.

Enjoy happy ideas and thoughts. Express them in a humorous way. Learning to find a funny bone in everything you do is really a talent.

Know also when not to use humor but to be serious. When a serious issue presents itself, people do not appreciate a clown, but someone who deals with it appropriately. Nothing is more annoying than to have

Spiritual Dancer

someone laughing inappropriately in a situation when it is time for seriousness.

14. Looking Through the Eyes of Love

It was one of the most beautiful lyrics I ever heard, "since I found you, looking through the eyes of love" words written by Carole Bayer Sager. If we could approach our world in this manner, how wonderful we would feel. Even when dark moments park at our doorsteps, how much better would it be to be looking at every situation with love-colored glasses. What a difficult time disenfranchised emotions would have sticking to our armor.

Could our presence bring nothing less than fulfillment? Our greatest gift to this world is our unselfish love. In order for this gift to not be tarnished with lesser motivations, paint each day with the best ideas of loving. When you look through the world, what do you see?

Living those daily practices are hard. My father once told me that any man could walk around angry at the world. He felt it didn't take any discipline whatsoever to frown, sharing negative thoughts, and telling everyone how society put you down. It takes a commitment to smile at life's situations, speak in a positive manner, and live your life to your upmost abilities.

The Beatles wrote, "All you need is love". Growing up in the late 60's my parents felt it was better to have a good bank account and a solid education. Love was something that worked itself out. Our household was filled with discussions on how business gave ample richness to those fortunate enough to seize it. Falling in love or love of spiritual knowledge was needed but not at the expense of earning a living.

Even though my mother was the organist of the church for over 60 years, when I wanted to pursue a deacon's position in the church, she wanted me to examine my motives. She felt that I was too immature for understanding the responsibilities of church leadership. Going to church was a process of keeping her children out of jail, finding a marriage partner and making great business connections. Love your neighbor as yourself was fine if there was a fence between you.

After a few weeks, I realized she was right about my convictions. I was thirteen and not mature enough in spiritual awareness to commit to such a task. I decided to join another gospel singing group and continue my education.

Singing from the heart

Where did I begin to understand love? Deep within my spiritual journey I began to realize that love was an empty concept if you didn't practice some level of responsibility. Of course, at first I thought love was related to simply falling in love with someone. In high school like most teens I had several encounters with what I thought was love. Romantic love was perceived as the love that would conquer all things. I paraded the halls in my latest fashion outfits, spoke softly, humorously to several females and discovered I knew nothing about love.

In those teen years, I began to write poetry. In my poetry, I expressed my belief that only the poet is the true lover of life. A few of my poems were published. As my poetry started to reflect my maturity, I questioned if this was the only way to explore love. I started to reach for new ideas. Were the Beatles right? Was all you needed was love?

We sing about love, but do we really understand the concept of looking through the world with our love eyes. Not just romantic love was I searching for, but a deeper meaningful existence.

In seeking such a romantic high, I discovered several paths that might lead me there. I found answers in music. Songwriters such as Billy Joel poured their heart into each phrase.

The year I graduated from college, I put a musical band together, not just for artistic expression, but also to sing top-40's love songs. In the silent hours of the night, I composed love songs examining this world and taking on the laborious task of delivering it to a disco era audience.

Spiritual Dancer

Our band of rock heads consisted of music majors, poets, and an insurance underwriter. *Grace,* the band's name, performed love songs from every musical genre of the time.

We rocked away in private clubs, college halls, and in bars. For each performance, I wrote original songs to perform. My songs ended up at Warner Bros. Music. I wrote from every musical angle. I composed lyrics in English and German but even through a great effort, my songs were never published. Some might say I failed. I would say that love of doing what is inside of you and bringing joy to those outside is the reward in itself. In those years, I discovered the importance of love lyrics. Years later, my love lyrics would be covered by several magazines and my compositions would end up on the movie screen.

Watching people dance to your music, enjoying the beat, the cadence of sound, allowing them to forget their world for a moment, is pure spiritual motivation. Why do we love music so? It brings out a deeper, more primitive voice in us. It might be called the universal language, but it is our soul drifting into musical oneness.

My mother gave our family the gift of her musical talents. Even though rock and roll was never her favorite music, she taught every one of us the piano. My twin sisters for a brief period followed in her footsteps by playing for local churches.

Music has become a spiritual voice of comfort for me. It expands how I approach the world and how I listen to my heart. Even as my hands float over the keyboard my soul stirs with the awareness of an open door waiting. Not just waiting for inspiration, but for the all-knowing to touch me. As I write my lyrical musical notes, I explore a deeper meaning of love expression and for this talent of song, I am grateful.

15. When Do You Know You're Doing It Right?

Anyone learning the soul's path takes on a mountainous risk. There is a risk of getting it wrong. Are you willing to take that risk? Are you willing to take a traveler's journey to the unknown without material rewards, praise, or even acknowledgement?

The greater risk is you do nothing. An unexamined life leads to unresolved delusions. Taking a risk involves discipline and discovery. Most people live their lives as Thoreau mentioned, in quiet desperation. They grow up, marry, work, have children, buy a home, retire, and die. They never examine their life, never take an adventure and never question anything.

I grew up in a small town. Some of my neighbors and friends never left the little town even to go to the bigger city only 27 miles away. I knew once I graduated from college, I had to leave. It was more comfortable to stay. My family had built up a respectable name and the family business had been quite prosperous. Some members of the local community bombarded me with verbal assaults for even thinking about leaving. How could I be so stupid? What opportunities would life afford me when I had all the riches lying at my doorstep? Even my family had their doubts. My sister believed leaving the business to pursue a career outside of the family was going be disastrous for me. My parents tried to reason with me but it was my destiny to leave.

I took a risk. I sold my house painting business contracts to my father. I gave away my unwanted things, sold what I could and raised enough money for the bus trip to California to seek my fortune. I packed my private notes and books, sheet music, and clothes into two large trunks then jumped onto a Greyhound bus.

The risk I took became the greatest decision of my life. For several years in Los Angeles, I wrestled with hunger, unemployment, but never lacked the courage to continue. It was challenging for I had never lived in a big city. For all the years I lived at home, I never had to really look for a job. I worked for my father every year in the business until

Spiritual Dancer

I left. When I applied for a job in my hometown, I was hired because the employer knew my father. In the city, no one knew me. No one knew my family. I relished the idea of starting anew.

After looking for work for months, I found a job working for a pharmacy and rented my first apartment. In my apartment I slowly created my "Mind Lab". This was my place designed to further my studies. I purchased more books, wrote more music, essays, poetry, and published a small book. I had a sprout garden on my windowsill and grew fresh tomatoes between the apartment buildings. I experimented with self-hypnotism and explored neuro-linguistic system training.

I continued to take risks by practicing my new-found mystical knowledge. I encountered interesting associates along the way. No path is without its downfalls. By practicing my philosophies I gained greater exposure to failure. At each course, I tiptoed along the edge of illumination. How close would I come to failing all together? I had my armor ready. I kept my faith in a greater spirit than myself. I continuously surrounded myself in God's loving light and when the troubles came, it was like a *Bridge over Troubled Waters*.

Practicing creates the method of living. The risk is first in the knowing and then in the doing. If you are going to talk it, you really have to walk it. Learning to live your life by the dictums you believe is what separates the practitioners from the theorists. It is where the courage truly is. Keep in mind, it's a daily struggle to practice all you believe, but you must and take the risk.

How do you practice? In your own tutorage, you practice the topics given. Keep your ideas focused on doing just a simple task. For example, in your meditative practice try forgiving of a past incident that caused you a lot of pain. Try something a little less troublesome. You haven't built the internal strength to practice on an overwhelming task on your first try.

Begin with an easier task, like an ill word spoken to you by someone at the grocery store or at work. Focus on the pain and the hurt this feeling caused you at that moment. Then quickly while you are immersed in this feeling, concentrate on how much the greater mind loves you. Let your mind envelop the newest feeling of love. Surround yourself with so much love that you imagine your body is glowing. In that presence, forgive the hurt you felt by this person. In that presence, give them so much love from a greater source than yourself. In that presence, send them the warmth of your glow, and then release them to their greater self. In all matter of sense, let it go. Do not dwell with the feeling. Let it go.

Silence as a method of exploration

Guard your new-found spiritual knowledge with care. Not everyone will share your opinions and you might find yourself on the defensive before truly understanding it completely yourself. In any profession of study, you must first adapt the information to your abilities, commit the data to your mind, and ask questions to clear confusion after testing, supervision, and application. Consider this stewardship a merit badge in your alliance to commitment.

Our verbal world gives rise to our communication media being at the speed of digital megabits. We can't wait to share our ideas with others. Invitations go out to our friends. After just reading a few chapters in our lessons we have positioned ourselves as experts and determined to convince our companions that they have ventured down the road of destruction. If only they would listen to our teaching.

A vow of silence is reverend from several schools of mystic learning. Historically this method might be construed as a secretive organization, but I believe it's to keep the novice from spouting ideas they have yet to understand. It takes several years of study to begin to understand the ideas of mystical thought and several years to be able to instruct someone else. Even then, not everyone you touch will be able to absorb, respect, or even consider your ideas as truth.

There is an ego practice inside of us where we must convince our fellow beings we are right. We parade our ideas like wonderful cloaks around our shoulders and display them with upmost certainty. We deem our knowledge as wisdom and become dangerously pious in our attempt to brow beat our associates into our way of thinking. Our ego self will not accept the possibility we don't have the correct program.

In high school, a friend of mine was on drugs. He perceived his life to be hip. He slicked his hair back, wore all the latest fashion and hung around with all of the "in" people. Over the period of high school, his drug problem took hold of him until one night in the street he overdosed. His so-called drug friends left him for dead. He had an epiphany. His life turned around. He discovered Jesus and came to church every week. In his transformation, he studied the Bible, spoke in tongues, prayed everywhere, and became a new person. There was no one who questioned his remarkable change, yet there was a problem.

He challenged everyone and everything with his newfound life. His immediate insight left him void of substance. He was arrogant. He was intolerant of other spiritual paths, and his days were filled with arguments and irrational ravings. When our friendship became strained, I reminded him of a great teacher who spoke of love not confrontation. And though we may be right in spirit, we are responsible for loving one another regardless of their faith or what conscious level they are operating on.

What he failed to understand was he was still a novice. Yes, he received a wonderful gift of insight. The wakening along the road was miraculous, but he was an infant, he did not have the maturing of expressing it. He had to learn to humble himself and remain a servant, a student, and know that not all persons will accept his message no matter how divine he thinks it is.

Spiritual Dancer

Silence for a novice is required for its justification for further wisdom. At what level is silence not required? A Master once told his Zen students, "Those who speak do not know." Not every question requires an answer. Not every situation requires a conversation. At every level of spiritual growth, sometimes the best response is none at all.

16. Preparing for the Long Journey

My wife and I are preparing a vacation from our home in Panama to go to California. For our trip, we create a list of things to do like packing clothes, books, our private notes, taking our passports, California driver's license, and tickets. We try to think of everything. Since we decided to stay with friends, we made sure it was a good time for them as well.

The preparations we make for our vacations are stellar. What preparations are we making for our journey through life? In the course of our journey here on earth, we are grand about our education, our careers, our marriages, but we take little time to feed our minds for the long travels throughout our years. How have you prepared for your life's journey?

Life happens while you are waiting for something else. How many of us wake up in the morning and can't believe a month, a year, went by already? Some of us wonder what we did in that year. What were our accomplishments? If we are in school, or on the job, we evaluate our progress by the amount of our paycheck, or the degree we obtained. But how do you evaluate your spiritual growth?

Our material needs for the long journey is complicated by our need for instant gratification. In this journey we must be thankful to our spirit every day. Start with giving thanks as you gather your thoughts as you are waking up, give thanks for living, and move on with your day. In our wondrous adventure called life, our progress is determined by our dedication to our life line.

Claim the journey as your own

Make a commitment to yourself that this day is your day. Make an affirmation every day. Look at the example below. Give yourself permission to dance anyway you want. It's your journey. Go enjoy it.

Spiritual Dancer

Example of an Affirmation

In spirit I claim this day as mine own. In spirit I determine to continue my growth and I am blessed by the spirit that creates it all. The Almighty. I am not troubled, or deterred from seeking my higher self. I am blessed. I am empowered. I am at peace with my journey and it is mine to take.

And so it is.

(To say "And So It Is" acknowledges the blessing is already yours)

17. Living Well with Others

When we come into this life our interactions with our family begin to define who we are. We learn how to communicate, learn acceptable and unacceptable behavior, and learn about ourselves as we develop our relationships with our parents and siblings. No one can escape the psychological impact these relationships have on us. In our attempt to reason our way through life's situations, sometimes we are saddled with defensive attitudes which prevent us from seeing other possibilities and alternatives.

Searching this universal plane for companionship begins as early as childhood. First, we are surrounded by our siblings and learn how we communicate to get along. Being raised in a family of older or younger siblings affects how we communicate and develop our relationships beyond the family environment. We are socialized to get along with others.

We are conditioned to get along, and as children our family determined with whom we could socialize. In my family there were "those" people who lived down the road with whom we were not allowed to associate. As children we innocently asked why not and our parents answered, "they are the wrong kind of people". We start to learn that some individuals are not appropriate playmates.

Later such conditioning extended itself to other ideas of undesirables. As we matured into our teens, we got the impression that it might have to do with race, religious thought, political persuasion, and/or monetary assets. Something strange happened in our teens, we begin to question and challenge our parental constraints, step into those undesirable arenas, and make friends with the people who are considered to be bad people or undesirables. We are critical of our parents and think them as being too judgmental.

Are these rebellious outbursts from our spiritual self to extend beyond our comfort levels to reach out to others? In a recent *Psychology Today*, adolescence was described as out-of-control hormones. The brain is receiving so much information rapidly that the teenager is wired for rebellion. Our bodies at that age are reprogramming our DNA at such a rapid pace, we react to everything emotionally. It is no wonder the teenager or the younger individual challenges status quo because his hormonal input does not process the information properly. Our socialization during the teen years can be described as an awkward period of trying to understand the people around us and how to get along with them.

In my community, I played with most of the kids. We created our own games, laughed, fought about what side the baseball fell on, and challenged one another to participate in being the king of the mountain.

Our parents had their agendas. They monitored our activities. They made sure we were not eating the grapes from the neighbor's vines; we did anyway. We rode our bikes but limited to only in the neighborhood. Local backyard picnics between families were the norm. It was a gathering of kids and adults to communicate with each other, share ideas on various subjects, and extend the social network.

By the adults demonstrating they could live with one another, the kids picked up the cues as determined by the adults' behavior. There were few outbreaks of fights. Because the parents knew each another, disagreements among the children were at a minimum.

The adults were also able to temper their disagreements. By building avenues of communication, issues were resolved without hot-headed arguments. The neighborhood became a basin for networking and inter-communication.

Power depends on proper communication

Currently, we are bombarded by inappropriate behavior and communication. We can term these "sound bites". Sound bites in the pop culture are lyrical phrases that define an entire idea. The problem with our communication with others is we must first deal with the concept of our rules of engagement which might mean nothing to someone not growing up in our specific environment. Our second challenge is to overcome sound-bite verbalizations and to begin meaningful dialogue.

The first challenge, having our communication be a two-way street. It's not just the speaker but also listener. Within our sound-bite culture, we must continue to be an active listener with the person with whom we are communicating. Can they indeed envision what we are trying to say?

The second challenge is to engage in thoughtful questions. If for some reason you failed to achieve a certain dialogue maybe you are not asking the right questions. Once my parents punished me for an act I did not commit because they assumed the information someone had given to them was correct, no questions asked. Later they discovered the truth from our neighbors, but too late for me.

Rules of Engagement

My parents picked my childhood friends, or tried to, and insisted on a set of rules for play and communication. As silly as I thought they were I was being conditioned on how to get along with others. One of their rules was never to eat at anyone's house even if they offered, never use their bathroom and above all to listen and to obey the adult no matter what you were told.

It was a part of my socialization. Did I defy these rules? Of course, I did at some point, but in the community I grew up in, everyone connected to my parents kept us in line. I lived in the old saying, "It takes a village to raise a child."

In a business environment we are aware that certain behavioral attitudes give way to promotions. In any business environment there are certain mental attributes of learning that will constitute exceptional behavior. In such environments, the idea of advancement is determined on your adaptability to a certain extent to the application of rules.

Living well with others is a spiritual journey through the entrapments of cultural biases. Our training in our particular culture is pertinent to our understanding of how humanity functions. Getting along with others re-examines our patterns of growing up, our assessment of our value. And somewhere along the line we are also attracted to and love those who have patterns different from us.

Everyone you touch wants to be loved and be appreciated. Some have had some of the same experiences you have, but many have had totally different lives. The magic comes when you pierce through the outer layers of their humanity and see the God in them. Do not become frustrated when they reject your friendship, simply understand, they are on a solo journey of their own, and spirit knows what is best for them.

18. Investing in Your Psyche

Agreements for a better you are now formulated in your psyche. How do you know when you are on track? Will you find all that gold you are looking for? What great awards await you?

Living with very few subtle changes does not give you a perspective on how you are doing. Some changes will enter your life swiftly while others you might not even notice. It is like an artist who has practiced his craft for several years. The first lesson is the instruction of the craft which the artist polishes and achieves some academic qualifications. The artist continues his journey with trial and error. The artist believes that refining his methods will lead to the mastery of execution. The artist commits to what he is doing but cannot see the end result. The artist might plead with Spirit to get that one break, but nothing happens. Yet, this particular artist might put his art on hold, while he continues to pursue other aspects of his life. He gets married, raises a family, but he's never far away from his craft. His home is surrounded with creative energy, power, hope, and in some spare time, he creates.

One day he stumbles onto something outstanding, something he knows to be his best work, and a miracle happens. Can you define your spiritual experience with the help of this allegory? One day Spirit wakes you up and you realize that the long journey was not in vain. It's a gradual expression. It may be something that you have been working on for years, and within a second, it surpasses everything you have known before.

If you are like me, you have studied various philosophies and attended several seminars on self-improvement. From each one of these I walked away with new insights. I continue to pursue knowledge through friends and classes so that my own life does not plateau to mediocrity. But when will it hit you that you have "arrived"? The only one who will know is you.

Spiritual Dancer

The problem with some idea of what to expect are often confused with the sudden awakening myth. In the movie, *Oh God,* starring George Burns and John Denver, the writer capitalizes on the angelic myth that the Universal Mind descends to earth and helps you like a father to get through all that there is. The manly figures are with you in your sleep, initiate conversations for answers, offer helpful hints on how to run your life, portray there is something really great that exists outside yourself.

In our real world, it is just plain hard work. There are no great flags waving. We build our lives one step at a time. As we are waiting for something outstanding, we might miss what just looks ordinary. In daily living, watch that you do not miss out on things that might be important. That neighbor you were having problems may just not live near you anymore. How about that extra money you find in your wallet that you didn't know you had. And just when you thought you couldn't grow anything, for some reason, those flowers you planted last year are growing everywhere. Learn to appreciate the ordinary.

When you should discuss spiritual lessons with others

Realize that most people we love are on their own path. As crazy as that path might seem to us, it's theirs. If you must discuss anything, allow your friends to ask the questions. Field them the best you can with an understanding of where your friends are presently in their consciousness. To start talking about concepts that took you years to comprehend will not only overwhelm them but misdirect your best intentions.

Living with the Himalayan Masters

Direct experience is the highest of all ways of gaining knowledge.
All other means are only fragments.
Swami Rama,

Spiritual Dancer

If the purpose of your exchange is to share, then it has served its purpose. If the encounter is to change someone's opinion, then you will likely fail. It is why philosophies are built on personal journeys. An individual does not assume the suit of a new ideology because someone convinces them; it is because they are ready for it, already made a decision to do so.

In your spiritual hemisphere of experience, it is resolutions which bring you solace. Practice motherly temperament when discussing your ideas with others. Realize that not everyone will want to venture into your world simply because it seems to work for you. With so many people searching and stumbling upon some ponderous insight, they can't wait to expound. We as their next victims are caught in the trap of defending our views against the onslaught of information. In their passion to share they become tyrants of their ideology.

No one can lead you by the nose to a path that is justified for you. Wisdom falls to the individual minds who seek it. In your quest to expound be mindful of others living in a world outside of yours.

19. Creating your Power Space

I called it my "Mind Lab". Nothing really special, just a single apartment with various tools I used for my spiritual journey. In my Mind Lab, I had my books, notes, herbs, music and a quiet place to meditate. In my refrigerator I had various fruits and juices for periods of fasting. I kept incense for relaxation and had heavy curtains to close out light.

After work, I gathered my thoughts from the day and sat quietly in my apartment, feeling the presence of my body while slowing down my breathing. I learned about eventually tuning out my environment. I wasn't in the mountains nor a temple placed high in the Hollywood Hills. I was located in downtown Los Angeles. Helicopters normally flew over every few minutes reporting traffic or crime. Sometimes there were gun shots in the distance and my neighbors were noisy. If someone was arguing I could hear it. I could count my neighbor's footsteps upstairs while vacuuming her apartment. How do you create a powerful space with all this noise?

No happiness surpasses peace of mind.
(Traditional Buddhist Proverb)

Slowly, while meditating I became comfortable with the sounds of my environment. Gradually, I allowed my mind to focus on breathing. Listening to each breath as it escaped from my lungs. I was counting my breaths, concentrating on inhaling and exhaling. This method was the simplest way of quieting my mind.

Once an earthquake rocked our building while I was in deep meditation. Even though I heard the many footsteps fleeing the building, I remained in a comfortable meditative state; I sat quietly until the shaking subsided. Afterwards, I lit a candle and waited for everyone to return.

Create a time each day in which you can practice. Choose the type of meditation which works for you and experiment with various styles. Be patient with yourself and your practice.

20. Righteous Ignorance

Beware of those righteous souls who have found some feeling of content and spew havoc on the "unfaithful". Over the last few years, compulsive forces on this planet have led a war against those who are moderates. In religion and on the political front a war of attitudes has plagued the world with unsavory ideas that if you do not believe what they consider to be truth, you were condemned.

Nothing is more terrible than active ignorance.
Goethe

"Active ignorance" is the arrogance when individuals claim their visions to be absolute while condemning and sometimes eliminating opposite points of views. Not recognizing experiences of others destroys the fabric of truth. No one can process all there is to know about anything. Institutions war with each other over the establishment of what vision the populous will follow.

When I took a tour of the city of Seoul, South Korea, our tour guide gave us a brief history of their Buddhist monks. The monks became so powerful in the empire that the king began tearing down temples and killing priests. The monks' influence with the community enhanced their power even at points greater than the king. The king pursued the monks and if they were captured they were imprisoned or executed. To escape the king's wrath lots of Buddhist temples were moved to tops of mountains and caves. The priests had to seek refuge far from the king's deadly military.

Karl Marx understood the euphoria spiritual institutions have on the masses. He felt that people could easily become misguided and show a greater devotion to their churches than their government. Societies have recognized this connection. Throughout history governments have tortured, killed, crucified, maimed, poisoned and eliminated any faction of ideology or person that would usurp the power of the government.

Spiritual Dancer

Why has spirituality taken on such a role and how does this affect the way we should seek peace? Any person seeking the kingdom of wisdom should understand that ideas shape nations. In recent years in the United States, the government has been swayed by factions of society with one noble cause, to persuade the hearts and minds of Americas that if you did not believe in the accepted vision, you were un-American.

This is nothing new in the society of men. If history teaches us anything, societies use belief symbols to build empires. Once a belief is formulated, then it must become the norm. If you do not commit to it, then you are doomed by it.

Believe in your commitment to do well.

Our Universal Father does not need your permission to exist. The Mother of all things does not need to demonstrate to you her existence nor does she desire your validation. So, who needs spiritual approval? Do you?

Once you control the hearts of the masses you control their thoughts. Those souls must through attrition go out and control other souls. It is a pattern of our nature. If not, we would not have left those peaceful caves, waterfronts, mountains nor ventured anywhere. In the quest for better lands, more food, more whatever, we create our communities around our beliefs. In our pattern of cultural attitude, we invent our world.

Our eyes are focused on the heavens, but our lives are dictated by our beliefs. In building our infrastructures, educational systems, militaries, and our places of worship, all things must reflect who we believe we are. We are the best at driving ourselves to destruction.

In fellowship those who have found the spirit will endeavor to teach and instruct others. It will be painful for some, rewarding for others. In teaching our children, our friends, our loved ones, we begin to formulate our teachings to benefit the community in which we reside.

Do not assume dissemination of controlled spiritual lessons is a bad thing for without some regulation most knowledge would deteriorate over time. While this teaching is being absorbed by the believers and non-believers some would enlist this power of knowledge as a means to dominate others. Those who love feeling good about themselves has found spiritual, motivational lessons to be comforting and uplifting. Instructions and lessons are methods of socialization. Some teachers have used the divine knowledge to manipulate their students. This type of manipulation may cause students to question the teachings. As we are manipulated, our divine self-craves for independent thought.

If the student cannot embrace the teachings and desires a different direction, then he must have the courage to question the teachings and may need to take a path that enables him to stay positive and closer to Spirit. The battle begins with defining his beliefs which remain intact no matter what events arise in his life. His moral skin weathers all influences and he emerges as loving light in the sight of God.

My way is the only way
Is a sign of Righteous Ignorance

Preventing your good intentions from falling into this trap is to be mindful of living a giving life. Share with everyone, but do not defend or direct the course of these lessons. Once I spoke with a friend about the spiritual teachings I had learned, and he told me he had no interest in my ideas. I respected his opinion. I continued to live my life through my philosophies and he and I remained friends. When he would ask how I felt or derived at a conclusion in my approach to various problems, I shared my positive ideology. The way you live is the process.

In the following years I grew to appreciate our differences. I never tried to convince him that my way was the only way to live. My appetite for knowledge continued to mature. Even though my friend and I were traveling separate paths we acknowledged our uniqueness and remained friends. On various occasions, he would be the first to acknowledge that I am very positive in my outlook on life.

When his sister made her transition, he was out of the state; he called me and asked me and my wife to come to her service to stand by his side during his time of grief. He was appreciative of the friendships we had nurtured through the years and we welcomed each other as brothers.

21. Gather Your Bags, Let's Take a Short Trip

In traveling across country, I love stopping at the rest areas. I watch my wife take our little dog for a stroll across the grassy park. He runs around for a moment excited about the new environment. I get a chance to stretch my legs, breath in a little air, and take whatever relief I need.

Gathering your thoughts and taking a trip allows the comfort of knowing your spiritual master rides with you. Even if you stray away from your teachings, the Spirit does not stray away from you.

As I look up toward the sky as I travel, it remains constant. The same blue sky and the clouds I see in Panama are the same fluffy ones I see in California, Pennsylvania or Korea. There is no special place or occasion that will separate you from yourself or God.

An exercise in Visualization

For an exercise gather these empowering thoughts: Envision vacationing on some exotic island. Quietly meditate on the image where every need you have is instantaneously supplied. You stroll along the beach for hours. Your body glows from the sunshine. It is a perfect temperature. You can taste the fruits from the trees and feel the ocean waves lap upon your feet. And when you are ready to leave your island, a luxury cruise ship appears to take you anywhere in the world you desire. The cruise ship sails off into an endless sunset which seems to last forever.

Why is this exercise important? Each day brings new experiences and new challenges, but you can place your mind anywhere you want. Each time you take a step toward a new location or an adventure, remember the island where everything exists. This is your potential. Your Father travels with you. Your rewards are not in heaven they are now on earth resting inside of you.

22. Begin Your Healing Today

Concentrate your entire being on the thought of positive energy. Do not think about your condition or situation. Ernest Holmes often taught that thoughts become things. What you are thinking about the most starts to manifest in your life. Begin by thinking about all those wonderful thoughts you have about yourself. Keep them focused in your mind. Then release them and just watch your vacation begin. No more of those negative ideas weighing you down.

Healing begins when you start to create a better image about yourself in your mind. Let's imagine you are exactly where you want to be in your life. How would you feel? Gather that feeling into the core of your person. Allow the image to consume you. Allow this feeling to permeate your thoughts throughout the morning, your day.

Stay clear of Energy Vampires

Have you ever been around a person or a group of people that made feel drained after meeting with them? Do you have friends, associates, family that once you leave them you feel a little sick? I call these people "energy vampires". They are sucking the positive light from you. Believe in your heart that like attracts like. Birds of a feather flock together, meaning if you do not want downers in your life, change with whom you associate.

The Law of Attraction

In my early dating years, I believed I could rescue people. Unknowing to my conscious mind I was attracting my lower self. My dates were always in need of help. After my encounters with them, I felt weak, sick, and the relationships were always unfulfilling. I would admit to my friends that I wanted something different, but I continued to date the same type of person.

I wasn't alone. My friends were doing the same thing. We would gather later to whine and detail our woes to each other. My friend would complain about not finding a companion that shared his interests. He could describe completely the person he needed in his life. Then each of my other friends would do the same, each one giving a complete picture of the perfect mate.

What I noticed in all this conversation was that no one wanted to take a closer look at himself. In the dating process, we were attracting the exact opposite of our needs. We simply settled. We all wanted a positive, nurturing relationship but we always chose otherwise.

This is the law of attraction. You attract what you desire the most. The confusion is what you say you want may not be what you are thinking. For example, I might want a nurturing relationship but I desire a needy woman who I can feel power over. My unconscious mind records my more powerful thought, needy, and I'll attract a needy woman. This is why it's extremely important to examine your emotions, say and think the same.

I decided to concentrate on detailing exactly what I wanted in a woman. I drew up a list. Once the list was completed, it was over two pages and included everything from hair color to type of temperament. Before going on a date, I stuck to my list by eliminating undesirables who did not possess the traits on my list. My dating life grew more productive.

Find time to practice what you are learning

Da Vinci felt new knowledge had to be tested and applied. He was not content to just theory. Mystically speaking information alone is not enough. Take some time every day to practice the lessons you learn.

When someone entered my office screaming about something I didn't do, I practiced patience. Why practice? In my case, I know that I am not very patient when someone questions my abilities. I took several deep breaths, focused and listened to what was being said without reacting. The importance of any learning is in the implementation.

The importance of practice is to strengthen behavior. In the beginning of any new idea it must resonant in our hearts. We must believe in its power and afterwards proceed to make it a habit. In order for the habit to solidify it must be a conscious effort to reinforce the knowledge.

In training for a weightlifting contest, I knew I had to do a few things. I had to start lifting weights for one. Heavy weights. To begin, before work I would go to the gym around 5 AM and begin to lift light weights. For the first few weeks, I was training my mind to accept the routine of 5 AM practice. In a few weeks, my mind was accepting the process of me getting up early and going to the gym, and my muscles were now also ready for heavier weights.

This process lasted for several weeks until it was time for the contest. Through several years of understanding my body's mechanics and the routine needed to compete at local, state, and regional levels, I knew that I had to maintain my schedule for several weeks with great intensity without harming myself. After years of competition and sticking to a routine, I have brought home several awards and trophies. Practice creates habit. Habit creates discipline. When utilized as a spiritual lesson, wisdom is instilled. I have been competing since 1983.

Abraham Lincoln said, "Anything worth having is worth working for". It is always about working hard to achieve your inner goals, and the rewards are happiness.

Setback, upsets, miscalculations

How do I handle setbacks? Frustration is the killer of motivation. So many friends I have met along my path became disillusioned when they failed. Most of them have turned away from their goals and rush into a corner of despair. They gather around other individuals who reflect their disappointment and reaffirm the world is harsh and they have their "pity party".

Our teacher O.C. Smith did not want to get invited to anyone's pity party. He instructed us to avoid pity parties even if we were giving one for ourselves. Setbacks really are just life's way of letting you know you are really on the right track. Every great idea has to be tested against the waves of resistance. It will take determination or the concept will run out of gas. Sticking it out strengthens your spirit.

Keeping motivation close at heart is powerful medicine. It will help to steer you through the rough waters of doubt. Most people give up too soon after a few setbacks. Failures are what teach us about who we are and what we will become.

Harry S. Truman failed at several business ventures. One venture was an oil drilling business. He and his partner had been drilling for several months and didn't find any oil. Discouraged they abandoned the exploration. Years later it was discovered if they had drilled just a little deeper they would have struck a huge oil deposit. Truman had given up too soon.

The method of dealing with setbacks is to surround yourself with positive individuals. Build your own brain trust consisting of people who are achievers. Surround yourself with friends and associates who relish life's challenges and look for positive ways to confront them. It is one way to limit energy vampires. Energy vampires feed off your goodness, however, your brain-trust associates exude energy.

My father once joined a flyers' club even though he did not fly. In the flyers' club the members not only had their own plane but were successful businessmen and women. In the clubhouse, my father was impressed that their stories were never about how much money they were making but how they laughed about their missteps in business. Their conversations were around all the mistakes they made and how they learned from them.

Your failures are your life's teachers. They give you a better understanding of your world and the world inside of you. Any one of us attempting to change our lives or foster a new idea is open to setbacks and failures. The only way you can adapt to this environment is to keep learning about yourself. Gather those impressive associates around you and keep learning.

Bill Gates said in his book, *The Road Ahead,* "In a changing world, education is the best preparation for being able to adapt." Your education is your life's journey. Wisdom is not limited to books. It's in life's lessons. The spiritual world has an infinite amount of knowledge for you. It will enrich you and protect you from life's ups and downs and set you on the path to nourish your mind and spirit.

I love books. My mother would read to me when I was a baby. Once she felt I was old enough she taught me to read before entering kindergarten; I was about four. In first grade, I was reading at a high school grade level. My mother believed education was the safe harbor for her children's life. She would drag us to The Citizen's Library in our town, made us understand how to use the Reader's Index to find various books for us to borrow.

Through my senior year, I had borrowed so many books from the library and paid so many late fees, that Mr. Lyon, the director of library, wrote me a letter calling me one of Washington's most outstanding individuals.

Reading trained my mind to seek out information. It gave me the capacity to evaluate ideas and make them my own. To appreciate knowledge, I encounter various methods and techniques that allow me to seek wisdom beyond the bookshelves. My mother instilled in me the desire for learning. Through her gift I've been able to seek more than mere knowledge, but to utilize my reading enthusiasm to absorb wisdom from a variety of sources.

23. Ordinary Tales of Power

The Infinite Universe created you of itself. You are God in action. When you remove yourself from "separation anxiety", the idea that you are separated from God, then you can understand the enormous power you process. What causes separation anxiety?

If you believe that you are God in action, then you have an uninterrupted, grand source of power. You are not just an image of God, you are God in spirit. Your spirit is God and there is no other entity. All teachings are mirrors of the divine. These are the instructions that lead you to your true self. These are stepping stones to the divine. The spirit of God dwells in you.

There are so many paths that can be taken, as Jesus would remind us of many rooms in His Father's mansion. As we tap into this unlimited power, we understand the purpose of the lessons is to find the God in ourselves. That is how ordinary people can do remarkable things, because they have learned beyond the confines of their own limited minds.

My father told me a story of God in action. My father's family was extremely poor. They did not own a car or even a good horse. Just before dark my Aunt Sara, a young girl, left the house to walk into the nearest town for food.

Before leaving she would pray for protection. When she left the house, a huge dog followed her. He stayed on the opposite side of the dirt road and when she was in town, the dog disappeared. She felt protected. When she tried to show the dog to my father and her other siblings, the dog was never around. She was never attacked on that narrow, lonesome road, nor was she ever afraid because she felt that the great hound was always there to protect her.

How many of these stories have you heard? This is Spirit in action. In my own life, I have recorded several incidents in my journals. Once I lost the only keys my father had for our house and car. I had been a little careless playing with my friends. The family and I had looked everywhere for those keys in the car, the house, playground. They had disappeared. I asked my spiritual Father whom I knew loved me very much to help me find those keys. Just before darkness came, I opened our unlocked car and the keys were between the door and the seat in plain sight. No one could believe it having repeatedly looked in the car.

We are part of this wonderful power without limits. We've heard several stories and read the books but we seem to continually fail to understand the significance of the stories. Jesus gave us lessons in power. His teachings were to instruct us how to love others, but also how to expect and to tap into this unlimited source of power, this generator that is inside each of us. He asked us to remember that the Father does the work. The methods of practice he gave us in stories and prayer.

The only guidance to understanding is that you already have the knowledge to do great things. You possess it now; it is inside of you. The choices are yours on how to experience your God-self. What choices will you make today to further your gifts?

Gifts of Power

What gifts do you have to reach your optimal life? Do you have insight into your current understanding that you don't know how to explain? Have you ever met someone and knew what they were going to be like even before you knew who they were?

Every spirit on this planet has gifts. The gifts we see are easily recognizable. I have a gift for music. In my high school, I would win singing contests and would participate in various choir festivals at local, regional, and district levels. My vocal range went from a baritone to a high tenor. When I graduated from college, I started a rock band and sang most of the slow, love songs.

These are gifts from God and they are precious. Examine closely what gifts come naturally to you.

Spiritual Dancer

These gifts come effortlessly. Perhaps you have a green thumb, or you're a good cook, or a painter. For others it may not be as obvious but nonetheless you too possess gifts from God.

Meditation Breathing Exercise
Practice lowering your stress by counting your breath

Find a quiet place where you can be undisturbed. Get comfortable in a chair making sure your legs are not crossed. Back straight, eyes closed. Count backwards from 10 to 1. One represents the lowest stressful state. If you forget where you are and your mind begins to stray, that's okay, don't fight it. Simply bring your attention back to your counting. As you count each number, visualize the number before moving on to the next number.

After a few minutes, you count in reverse from 1 to 10 bringing your mind out of meditation. Open your eyes. Feel the relaxed state of mind you just created. Repeat this exercise as many times as you desire. If for any reason you find it hard to concentrate, consider it part of the practice; do not become discouraged. Sit for as long as you can then increase your sessions over time.

24. Relationships Built on Love

I have always believed that I wasn't looking for someone to make me happy. I was already happy. I also felt that it was not my responsibility to make someone else happy; that was their responsibility. In my dating life, it became apparent I was looking and searching for the wrong idea of love. In a huge city like Los Angeles, one could get lost in the image of love and become a little ignorant on how to pursue it.

Like attracts Like
The Law of Attraction

Grouping of members are comparable to vibrations of individuals or beings seeking to be with each other. Birds, lions, cows, all seek the companionship with their kind. It is similar to the spiritual path within us. Even on a sub-conscious level we are making choices to associate with like individuals and circumstances. We create an environment which attracts like in kind.

Several of my single friends over the years have expressed that they were not happy in their love lives. Even though they seemed to be practicing a spiritual path, they commonly forgot their teachings when it came to finding a love companion.

Marianne Williamson in her lectures based on *The Course in Miracles* informs us that sometimes we attract a person we *desire* then try hammering them into the person we *need.* In other words, there are certain qualities we like, but those other things that come with them we want to change. We imagine a perfect relationship which is not with the person we are dating. With the image in our minds, we try to force the person into the golden picture frame of what we think would be our perfect relationship.

An example of this is when a friend of mine was dating a beautiful bartender. He was attracted to her outgoing personality and her sense of humor, but as time went on he was always frustrated over her lack of interest in books, culture, and other things that he enjoyed. "She just doesn't read", he said. I mentioned that when he was dating her he wasn't looking for a reader. He was attracting the person which fulfilled a desire, his thoughts. He needed to think deeper and want more than one trait on his list of characteristics that he defined for his perfect relationship.

Finding a soul mate is a gift from the Universal Mind

Surviving the dating world is a challenge. In our search for our spiritual partner we make numerous mistakes. Our experiences are fraught with pitfalls and disappointments. A true soul mate is a gift from God. It is a miracle in today's media-driven environment to be able to tune out the misinformation of true love and to examine the deepest aspect our needs.

We must clearly define what we want in our life partner and be willing to fail; not to be afraid to fail. Living in the Hollywood scene I learned that not everything is what it appears to be. Personalities can be faked. Honesty can be extremely hard to find.

What is the perfect relationship?

What really do you seek in a relationship?

If your notions are undetermined, loose, then you attract the same. If you are thinking about outside beauty instead of spiritual awareness, you will attract those limited to good physical attributes. When all your friends, relatives, associates fumble through their relationships, where can you see some examples of true love and great relationships? Even the best of relationships, by psychologist standards, teeter on destruction. So, how can we as spiritual students attempt to outwit this phenomenon?

I must confess that I have in earnest dated a lot. In my own trials, I found my years of dating led me to understand that most people never stop to examine what they are doing. My experience has taught me that most people including myself are quick to blame the partner, the city, the current economic situation for failures in love.

Spiritual Dancer

Men and women are equal parts of the same Spirit. In the course of your life, the spiritual world sends to you life lessons. In marriage, as in dating, we yearn for completeness. There's a void to be filled. We yearn for love but maybe feel we can never really get it because we don't deserve it. Unconsciously we "settle" and accept incompatible partners because we are wrestling with the knowledge that we really don't know what we want or need. Our spirit knows what we need. We may believe we are not worthy of love so we continue to make the same errors over and over again.

How many people will not leave a bad relationship or an abusive one because they don't think they could do any better? Is it because they don't believe they have the ability or self-love to deserve anything better?

Companionships are the hardest of all relationships to maintain. In our first introduction to each other, we are spellbound by what we see. During the course of dating our companion says the right things, orders the right meal, wears the right suit, and laughs at everything we say. However, there is something that disturbs us about this relationship. We can't put our finger on it, but something is just not right. We ignore our feelings, our intuition and continue anyway.

After several additional dates, a pattern emerges. Those tiny character flaws mount. In our desire for a relationship, we overlook them and pretend they don't exist. In observing other couples, we determine that everyone has issues. We are convinced happiness is a fantasy. Our image of happiness eludes us. We retreat into our lives blinding our spirit to what could be if only we had the courage to make better choices.

Spiritual Dancer

Understanding dating patterns

Dating is practice for marriage. Examine the qualities of your partner for just a moment and determine if this is the person you want to live with for life. Is this someone you can grow with spiritually?

After my first, short-lived marriage, I realized that I needed better criteria for future dating. I began to ignore my buddies and their bad advices and ventured on my own. I began to work on me. I wanted to turn myself into the best candidate for the best partner. What in my life needed changing? What did I need to improve?

This process took over two years. I closely studied all the women I had dated, examined their traits, and reviewed my dating ritual. I then mapped out a different approach. I kept notes and made adjustments. I watched how couples interacted with each other at malls and wrote down my observations. I asked questions from my female friends. I listened to their comments and took notes.

How could I incorporate this into my life? A relationship is built on appearances of truth. Not just about the other person, but how you want to be perceived. I found that I didn't have to work to get anyone to accept me; I had to work on being honest about me.

I had to put my research into practice. My first test came when a woman at work asked me out for coffee after work. I suggested a place close to work because of our work schedule. As we tried to work out the details, she started making excuses: something came up, the café was too far, might have to work late. In the past, I would allow my entire schedule to be manipulated and be accommodating. I realized through self-evaluation that I didn't need to do this, so I politely suggested maybe we should try another time. We never did and I was better off for it.

Each date for the next few months was recorded in my notes, and I evaluated the date on the merit of her personality and character. I entered every dating situation filled honestly and did a quick assessment of the relationship. When it just didn't measure up, I moved on.

Spiritual Dancer

One day I realized that I had outlined exactly what I wanted in a partner. Most people do not know what they want in a partner and keep blaming the other person for failing to measure up. My list was two pages of requirements. Anthony Robbins inspired this method in his *Personal Powers* tapes. I detailed it down to height, hair color, and educational level. Through understanding what I desired, the energy went out to the Universal Mind. When I met Karen, she had every characteristic that I wrote on those sheets; we were married within a year.

Through the eyes of spirit

You don't need someone to make you happy if happiness resides in your heart. The idea of the spiritual relationship is to share the happiness you already have inside. If you have to find happiness outside of yourself, you will have a void in your heart that may never be completely filled. Happiness and content find an equal representation of itself in Spirit. You are Spirit.

Make yourself whole, be happy with yourself then ask the Universe for your ideal mate. Be specific about what you want. Once that person enters your life, acknowledge it as a miracle from God. Work every day on sustaining your relationship. Do not let jobs, children, mortgage payments, life's issues get in the way of continuously loving and knowing your spiritual mate, your special gift which God has given you.

25. Walk with Humility

Let someone have a moment of your time to express himself without you interrupting before he can complete his thought. In our spiritual journey, we can become boastful of our knowledge of mystical concepts. Many of us might fall in this category of expressing our newfound wisdom.

My family is filled with ultra-ego personalities. Before you can complete your statement you are interrupted. At a family gathering while conversing with my father, I had to stop to remind myself that there were others in the room who might want to join in our conversation.

God gave us two ears and one mouth, so we would spend
Half as much time talking and twice as much time listening

The hardest lesson for someone as talkative as I am is to learn to be a good listener. It starts with allowing others to have a say; not always dominating the conversation, as I did. Too many times our teachers are trying to show us the way but we talk over them. In *The 7 Habits of Highly Effective People* by Stephen R. Covey, the author mentions the successful habit of active listening.

The art of active listening is being engaged when someone is talking; really listening. When conversing, pause occasionally; take a breath. Allow your ego to be present but not dominating. Enjoy honestly listening to the person talking. You can prepare your response to give an appropriate time. When you notice you are dominating the conversation, step back, ask questions and return to actively listening. Stay attentive.

Being humble allows you to listen with your heart

The act of being humble is in knowing that you do not have to be the center of attention, keeping your desires in check and not flaunting your achievements. Be thankful for the smallest of miracles and treasure your gifts. Finding moments to honestly praise others; you don't want to be condescending.

In your practice allow others to have center stage. Get to know them through words and thoughts. I come from a family and have friends who I think have never heard of sharing the stage with others. They are afraid someone will snatch them from their podium and interrupt their agenda.

You are practicing perfection

As students of life we are preparing for a higher level. Our constant goal is to learn. We are practicing to be more "Christ like". As students we strive to be better, to do good things, to help others, to be the best we can be. We acknowledge we are being molded by the great *I Am.*

26. Laugh More, Worry Less

Norman Cousins understood the power of laughter. Audiences and readers love a good joke. Having a great sense of humor is a wonderful combatant against depression.

Is depression the enemy?

As mentioned in other chapters about stress being registered on the skin, we also know it is recorded in the bones and the organs of our body. Depression robs you of your abilities to face the world. Depression is a downer. It is confusion that leads you away from your positive energies. Use the power of I AM to help combat depression. Repeat to yourself or aloud positive things about yourself, such as, "I am intelligent. I am attractive. I am a good friend. I am a good worker."

Words have power. Never say negative things about yourself or your condition, even in jest. There are challenges enough in life without you helping it. Fight off those negative voices and forces in life. Shake it off. Do not use the wrong I AM, like "I am dumb". This only helps the negativity take over. Using faith look forward to what you want your conditions to be, say, "I am creative. I am a strong. I am well off. I am blessed." Know that God planted seeds into each one of us to use to our full potential. We have God in our corner. We are God's masterpiece.

The greatest spoiler of depression lies in daydreaming. Daydreaming on future ideas can zap depression of its power over you. Dreaming of the projects you want to do and the people you want to meet permeate the spirit with renewed energies. Depression is never eliminated so when it emerges immediately reject it and replace it with positive thoughts.

Scientific evidence presents numerous papers on the topic of stress and illness. While the medical world encourages the use of drugs, the mystical spiritual world preaches of having a Joy-Filled life. Focus on God. Fill

Spiritual Dancer

your day with people, things, activities that bring you
joy. Believe that your spiritual Father has never left you.
Practice your faith. When depression comes knocking
at your door don't acknowledge it, envision the world
you would create for yourself.

27. Angels Abound

In 2008, my mother forgot about the pan on the stove and caught the house on fire. The story about her plight hit the evening news and the local newspaper. Her weathered face was plastered on the front page of the local newspaper. She appeared confused and incoherent.

My mother was diagnosed with dementia. She would walk the streets and alleys in her mental state, lost. She was unaware of passing cars or the kind person who sometime would take her home. Two angels watched over my mom when her house caught on fire that fateful day; they pulled her out of the fire and saved her life before the fire department arrived.

Angels are everywhere

In our lives are we looking for miracles to happen? Are we looking to the heavens for angels? Where are they?

There are angels everywhere.

When my mother was walking the streets and coming home late at night, there were angels watching over her. They made sure she got onto the right bus or simply brought her home. When she had money in her pocket the angels made sure she was never robbed. Our family never knew who these angels were but even now I hear stories of how my mom was protected by the community that she had dedicated so much of her love and life.

Later, I discovered those angels who pulled her from the house. One of the men told me that he had to lift my mom onto his shoulders and carry her out. My wife and I thanked them for saving her life.

Angels are everywhere and come in all shapes and sizes. They are the miracles we have been hoping to see.

This inspired a poem I wrote which first appeared in *Red Owl Magazine*:

What if

What if my angel is the one I abused

Spiritual Dancer

the ex-lover I thought I used
or the rumors I spread that were untrue
what if my angel was you

One late night on my motorcycle, I drove through a red light at one of the busiest intersections in downtown Los Angeles. It wasn't until afterward that I realized what I had done. I quickly looked around and saw there was no sign of any cars on the road. Even though I was late for work, I pulled over to the side of the road, and thanked my Spiritual Father for this miracle.

Miracles happen every day. Keep your eyes and mind open to seeing the miracles.

28. Knowledge in the Absence of Thinking

Often when we stop to gain knowledge it is done with prejudice. We absorb only what we believe will be relevant. In the course of that process we must do as spiritual beings: not to equate our reasoning to just logical thinking but also to the belief in things that do not always manifest.

Some of us can repeat great poems without knowing its meanings or recite mathematical formulas without understanding the purpose of the equations. Once in a business meeting with upper management, I quoted some managerial procedures from my recent business studies and asked why we were not pursuing that path. My regional manager who held a master's degree in Business quickly responded by saying that even though that was a wonderful theory, it was not field tested. He mentioned that even though I understood the material I failed to assess the appropriate application for it.

You need to field test your philosophies. Are they really working for you? In our life experiences, we seldom end up with the opinions we started with. Ever notice how our ideas and opinions change as our environmental circumstances change? You redesign your life to adjust to the changing situation. What really is working for you?

In your field testing experiments allow yourself to be an observer as well as a participant. This may give way to new information, new knowledge. Keep an open mind. I find that once certain information is removed from our minds, our minds are then open to new ideas, perspectives that we've never considered.

29. Distorting Information

In Charles J. Fombrun's *Turning Points,* he discusses how often information is distorted and how strategies are needed in corporations to challenge existing views. He writes, "It often surprises people to learn that the human brain systematically distorts information and routinely biases our decisions."

How often does our knowledge become a false perception of reality? Can we pretend to understand the emotional state we experience when we gather our data?

The joyous revelation is that we cannot always depend on our memories to be accurate, even with a shared experience. My siblings and I have a totally different memory of some events as we grew up. I remember my father playing basketball and riding bikes with us. One of my sisters recalls that dad was always working and never remembers him playing any games with us.

Anthony Robbins might label such memories as "emotional triggers". Emotional triggers are laden with extreme feelings at the time of an experience. A song plays on the radio and it reminds you of when you danced with your first date in high school; the song is a trigger. Every time you hear that song memories electronically etched into your mind elicit a certain feeling. What you might not remember is that she stepped on your toe while dancing. But on that day this song projects a sweet, emotional feeling.

Information becomes more distorted when it suits our purpose or protects us from harm. Some memories are blocked out completely, such as being verbally abused and humiliated by a bully. Information tied to those memories could be too painful to recall.

Begin fresh without delay

Your actions taken in small amounts toward a goal of self-achievement will weed out unwanted and useless data. Make that commitment to yourself each morning to do your best in whatever comes your way.

30. Conversations with The Great I AM

In your mediations, let there be peace in your soul when you sit outside of yourself and speak to Spirit. With our understanding of this Spirit, cast your face over the waters of your life and ask to participate in a greater understanding.

How do you begin to communicate with The Almighty? When at work in California I would have lunch inside my office, turn off the lights and dream. Dreaming is a form of quiet ideas running through your mind so that Spirit can enter. Closing my eyes at the height of hectic activities during my day was my method of stopping and praying, concentrating and envisioning what God might want to say to me. Sometimes this was just a random act of listening.

Random acts of talking to God

Every morning I would get up and take long walks through our neighborhood in Pasadena watching the sun comb its way through the trees. Letting my mind filter out my own uncertainties, I talked to Spirit to enlighten my path, "Show me the way to be more intuitive about my studies and allow me the opportunity to love abundantly."

Lessons are learned this way. There are no rules, no special, right or wrong ways to talk to God, only your way. Our parental spirit resides inside of us. Communication formulates as our temperament expresses itself. Some days you are singing in the shower, praising; some days you are sitting in your car on a busy city street, praising; as long as you realize this wondrous Spirit is everywhere, there is no need to limit yourself to an environment.

Growing up in a Baptist church, my mother being the organist, my grandfather a deacon, there were strict rules on prayer. As an adult I was able to determine for myself how I would pray and incorporated my own introspection on the subject.

Spiritual Dancer

I believe we all have a direct line to God. Your Spiritual Father is on speed dial. You do not need a special invitation. Dial it. Begin the conversation as if you are speaking to an old friend. The journey should be a joyous one.

31. Being Joy-Filled

What happens when we wake to a fearful day? How many times have you had a restless night of sleep only to wake to more issues you have to deal with? Does it become harder for you to praise the greater Spirit when you face the world or a task which is overwhelming?

My joy-filled life does not come without effort. My latest challenge is living the words that I write in this book. As my journey continues to unfold, it becomes easy to write the words, but I have to live the life as it is the ultimate goal.

In the winter of 2007, my sisters and I started having meetings and discussions about taking care of our parents. It became a daunting task because of the emotional entanglements of societal responsibilities and personal ill feelings within the family. We started out with a plan for honest communication with each other and with Aging Services and Protective Services. The plan entailed removing our parents from their home which was unlivable and placing them into a facility that could take better care of them because they refused to live with us, their children.

However, the plan came with its complications. First, Protective Services already assessed mom as being mentally incompetent and requested that I assume guardianship; my sisters wholeheartedly agreed. The only reservation I had was that I lived in Panama, but my sisters agreed to keep an eye on our parents since they lived locally and to inform me of any issues requiring my attention. The second obstacle was to determine where my parents would be located and the condition of the facility; Protective Services would offer recommendations. My wife and I left our home in Panama for a court hearing in late December for me to assume guardianship, with a plan to return to our Panama home within a few weeks. What occurred in the next few months was a chaotic spin through the governmental hang-ups and family trials that neither my wife nor I could foresee. What should have taken a few weeks, the governmental bureaucracies tied our hands for months. The family splintered off into non-speaking parties. This is still a mystery today how this happened. We all agreed on the course of action, so what happened? Old sibling rivalries? I did not think so. We had to rely on the kindness of friends to watch over our home in Panama, and take care of our dog, Toby, while wrestling with a boat-load of issues. Our friends in the States invited us to stay with them for as long as we needed, suspecting it would take several months while we labored over my parents' dilemma. Where was the joy-filled life? How could I claim that goodness was all around me when all I saw was discontent and chaos?

Happiness is your choice

To say that when tough times come it's still easy to see things "in the light" is misleading. It takes a concerted effort to stay positive and joy filled. By staying "in the light" throughout the madness, I saw the winter ice melt away, the spring brought daffodils blooming outside, and the weather warming. When I was the least joy-filled, I watched the deer jump through the winter snow and play as if God meant for nothing else for them to do. In our frantic encounters to shuffle through with my parents' debt of thousands of dollars, we discovered new friends, new business associates, and a new director-producer for my scripts.

While one family member refused to talk to me or to even discuss my parents' condition, I had another and newfound friends who allowed me to vent my frustrations. I also heard some untold stories of my family's history from others in the community. At every turn, if I looked closely enough, my angels were there watching over me even when I didn't feel so joy-filled at that peculiar moment.

When you fall from your healthy mindset of spiritual abundance, you are not a bad person. Allow Spirit to steer you back home. Your joyous journey sometimes leads to unsuccessful events. You discover painful moments or a history of unresolved issues will pop into your current existence. You have done nothing wrong if you feel slightly off your game. It's just life telling us that some things are not meant for us to control. However, we can choose how we react to it.

How did I respond? Angry and resentful, at first of course. Then I remembered how blessed I was to have loved ones in my life doing everything to help us. We had friends who were honestly happy to have us stay in their home for several months, not ever wanting us to go home. We had friends in Panama who watched over our home and dog, and we had friends in the California who wanted us to stay with them as long as we wanted.

Karen and I had each other. We needed time each day to remind ourselves of our teachings and our commitment to our own happiness. We knew there was a reason for this experience. What did we do? We took our commitment to each other seriously and had faith. We took it a day at a time, dealt with each issue as it came up, and made the best of the experience. We certainly experienced a lot of new things!

Find those strengths in your life that reflect who you are and what you are. In my own journey I went from a single man to a dedicated husband. I retired young, purchased property in another country, and redefined what it meant to be a loving son, husband, brother and friend. It was not an easy journey, however, each step along the way I believed that Spirit was greater than any challenge I would face. My joy was in the doing and the discovering. When I determined my goals were designed for my own projections on life, I discovered a deeper meaning of my desires and understanding.

It would have been easier for me to take my frustrations out on the family members who I felt were not supporting me or the government agencies that lost my mother's files. It would have seemed justified to become angry with family and friends who didn't understand what my wife and I were going through and lash out at the organizations that were unhelpful. Instead we chose faith. We remained patient.

No matter how popular the notion, your comfort should not cause discomfort to others. My wife and I have suffered some business setbacks because we refused to build our lives on the suffering of those around us. We sometimes go out of our way to forgive those who have wronged us even at the cost of losing money, family or friends. I live with the conviction that happiness in our lives will not be built on the misery of others.

32. Let Love be your Guide

Love only makes me remember,
it alone makes me alert.
Leonardo da Vinci

No lesson in life is greater or harder than love. It must be the basis of whatever discipline we surrender ourselves. Love is worthy of your total mental consumption. Be in the spirit of love. Begin your day by having a conversation with your higher self with songs of love. Make this your goal or your objective.

How do you practice this? Josh Groban sings a song, *"You Raise Me Up"*. The theme of love raises us up to stand on mountains, walk on stormy seas and to be more than we can be. We are not bound, for love frees us.

Turn on your heart light

Start by allowing your ego to occasionally drift away. Listen to a quiet voice inside of you. If you need a reminder, look outside to the clouds. Start dreaming about the perfection in you. Let your love overtake you.

Have love sessions with yourself. I have verbal conversations with myself about what great things I have done. Remind yourself often of God's love for you. Dance feeling His love around you like mighty armor. Imagine this armor is your shield against all negative energy, all self-hate and nothing can penetrate it.

Enhance your surroundings to reflect your inner peace. Read uplifting books, share laughter with your friends, turn off the negative news and embrace your joy.

Stop and pray about your desire not to hurt one person in your approach to your life. The path of lovingness is a difficult journey. It is not just a method of appearing to be loving, but a conscious action of it.

Spiritual Dancer

No one said it would be easy, but most of all enjoy the dancing journey. As a child we played upon the grounds and in the mud without thought of how many germs there were until we took biology class in school. As a child we shared our drinking water with others never thinking how we could be spreading disease through our mouths. As a child we danced without restriction and we loved as if there was nothing stopping us.

Stress Happens

Every mystic searches the world for teachers. Stress is our finest teacher. When I find myself in a stressful situation, I take time away from the battlefield. In my mental course of action, I become inactive. While others are pounding away at the rock, chipping away at the problem, I am determined to dream beyond it.

Our spiritual Father does not bring us to situations to fail. In the course of human journey our goal is to learn and to believe that this is just another step in our spiritual evolution.

How can this be done?

Identify the problem. Once I took a job working for a credit company. Within a few months I realized I had made a drastic mistake. Even though I was making money, the company was not a good fit for my personality.

Instead of listening to my inner spirit, I continued to work. I was not a quitter after all! I began to develop migraine headaches, uncontrollable weight gains, sleeplessness and peaks in high blood pressure. My performance was dismal and eventually I was asked to leave. I actually thanked my boss for firing me!

I was out of work for several months but it was the best thing for me. As soon as I was let go, my weight and blood pressure returned to normal and no more headaches. In trying to outthink my nature I was developing health issues.

33. Happiness is What We Live For

No one can live your life any better than you. Happiness is your spiritual right. Unconditionally. As long as you are not demanding others to live as you live then you are on the correct path.

Benjamin Franklin in his pursuit of his happiness created the Juno group of businessmen and scholars. He wanted to connect with various individuals who shared his view but also to develop vital connections for advancement. He was establishing a means to his happiness and fulfillment.

What organization, friends, associates do you belong to further your development?

We are social creatures. We are defined by the company and associations we keep. What you want to do is surround yourself with positive people. Your associates are reflections of you. If someone were to look at your friends, in their eyes they would see you.

Maintain positive learning positions with your friends. If the conversations begin to take a negative spin, interrupt the pattern and switch back to something positive in nature.

Social support research offers several theories in maintaining and sustaining good health. In the book, *The Healing Brain* by Robert Ornstein and David Sobel, it suggests that society's complexities of our communal interactions enhance our immune systems and combat diseases. Other research lends further testimony to encouraging the correct relationships to extend life, such as married men live longer than single ones. Your spiritual communities should consist of pro-active people who enjoy your company. Rid yourself of those who engage in negative thoughts and stimulate only bad feelings.

34. Document Your Happiness -- Journal Writing

It's never too late to begin journaling. What can journaling do for you? You can document your progress. You can study and examine your spiritual growth. When discoveries occur in your life you can express them freely in your journal.

You do not have to be a writer to document your happiness. When I first started my journal in 1967, I was recording daily activities. When we purchased our first horse to ride on the open street and my sister fell off, I recorded the experience in my journal. I wrote about our adventures of taking out the backseat of our old car, pushing the pony into the back of the car, in which he walked in freely, and my dad driving the car to the farm with our pony's head sticking outside the window.

Our neighbors watched with amazement as our pony trotted into the back of the car each weekend to return to the farm. Everyone who witnessed this event couldn't believe their eyes. My personal journal captured these moments.

When you record your thoughts and feelings, these are for you alone. It's a moment in time to reminisce. I never write for anyone but myself. I usually record my ideas, dreams, books I've read, thoughts about everything, places I've visited, relationships, and sometimes even things to do in case I forgot. There are no rules to journaling.

I get joy from recording things and now I have several journals reflecting how I have matured. I wrote of things happening in my life, good things, fun things, some were spiritual in context, others were not. For the hard times I praised the Spiritual Father as I overcame them.

How should you start?

Each person has a different need. I first started as a child by buying a small note pad which I drew some ideas about how I thought Jesus should look like. I also jotted down my ideas on math and chemistry, ideas for inventions, and drawings – cartoon characters and some architecture. I found the notepad a little too limiting for me, so I went to the store and purchased my first diary. On each page there were dates and I had to write in the diary at certain times. I purchased a five-year diary in 1973 and kept it until 1982. I found writing on a specific day extremely confining and a lot of wasted pages when I missed days. Each page had five small spaces for your entry. I would take up about a paragraph for each day for five years.

Along the way from 1965 to 1982, I wrote down my concerns in various notebooks and journals specific to the topics at hand. If I was creating music, I created notebooks for my compositions. In 1978 I started a house painting business and kept various business pads and accounting notebooks of my expenditures. I copyrighted my poems and essays from my notebooks. I have more than one pad for recording.

Keep your journal open and simple. My wife decided to start a journal. When she missed a day, she became frustrated and stopped. Do not become discouraged when you are not writing every day. I guarantee there will be no demerits given to you for missing a day of journaling.

I love artist pads purchased from bookstores like Barnes and Noble when they had a sale. The pages are blank. I can draw on them and I never have to worry about meeting some date printed on a page. Over the years, I have switched from buying diaries at the local supplies stores to artist pads because it fits my needs better.

What should you write about?

Anything you want to. Make your journals as personal as you desire. Begin with just recording what happened during the day and then push your creative muscle to record other ideas. Most of what we know about historical individuals comes from their letters. David McCullough's book on *John Adams* derives some of his biographical prose from Adams' letters to Abigail his wife and from his journal.

I gain a great deal of satisfaction watching my growth over the years. Pulling out my journals and re-reading passages that I wrote several years ago, helps me to understand where I was and how I have grown. I frequently do this periodically.

If you have your adventures recorded, what a wonderful heirloom to leave to your loved ones. In families, history gets lost because of bad memories or shame. The real shame is not knowing your family's history. We should recognize that what happened was the past but nonetheless it happened. It would have been interesting for me to know more about my mother's history, for she shared little. History no matter what course it takes belongs to the future, the children.

I found that recording assisted me in my progress through life. I examine what methods are worth pursuing and what methods to leave behind. The knowledge I gained has been invaluable. Knowledge versus intelligence is in the application of knowledge. Anyone can gain a lot of information over the course of their lives but applying it is true intelligence. Knowledge forces ignorance to take a different path and be eliminated.

I've been able to study my writings and my progress from grade school, high school, college, throughout my life. How I have matured! My journal revealed how I changed, how I'd grown and what ideas I wanted to work on for the future. I recorded my feelings and my setbacks, and how I thought about those things. It also contained my prayers, meditations, and my acknowledgment of my relationship with God.

Journaling is witnessing your growth. To this day in my notepads, I am able to record unlimited ideas. My thoughts, joys and frustrations spread across a canvas where there are no judges, nor witnesses to impede my expression. I dare to know more about myself. I challenge my own thoughts for personal betterment and become my own champion.

35. Spiritual Dancing with Others

Instead of teaching others what a wonderful journey your studies have taken you, show them with your love. When I was in Campus Life, a youth Christian organization, at the end of our teachings we sang a song, *"You will know we our Christians by our Love"*. It was a wonderful way to end every sermon. In our *City of Angels Church,* we would end each of Dr. O. C. Smith's teachings with a song, *"Let there be peace on Earth and let it begin with me."* This would choke up my wife as she felt the power in those words.

Spiritual dancing with others engulfs a lot of love and bit of non-preaching. It warrants reminding that we are not here to explain how God works; we are here to dance in the spirit of love. Resist the temptation for preaching.

The price of greatness is
responsibility over each of your thoughts
Winston Churchill

A great dance is one where you are learning as well as sharing. Never overstate your intentions, but consciously listen to each word and each phrase without interruption. The art of the dance is to interpret the time and step accordingly. It does not matter who is leading, but who is dancing.

Every dance is different. My wife and I live throughout the year in Panama. More because of the cultural differences between our countries than the language, we often became frustrated. One Panamanian friend let us in on a little secret. He said we had to learn the dance. In Panama there was a certain way of doing things that are quite different from the United States. We had to learn to stay in time with their beat, their way, not the way it worked in the U.S. We had to learn to dance, The Panamanian Way.

This advice was reinforced by our other Panamanian friends. We listened. We adapted to the mindset of the culture we were in. Our lives became easier and abundant as we stayed in step with Panamanian time. In Panama, we learned how to dance, and we thank our friends for sharing their wisdom with us.

The hardest task is when you like to dance but others do not. Dance anyway. You are Spirit and Spirit does not need a reason to give itself. Try not to take this personally. Shakti Gawain in her book *Living in the Light* said, "We forget our spirits, believing we are just our personalities".

Never forget you are Spirit dancing.

36. Balancing through Life

My dance is a dance of love. Love of life. You don't dance because your feet are on fire; you dance because you are enjoying your abundance. Yes, you have an abundant existence. Everything the Universe wants you to have is within your grasp. All you need to do is reach for it.

Finding the right dance to sway to is our life's mission. Gather your mind to the commitment of traveling well along the road of life. A strategy of your personal advancement lies in the avoidance of misguided energies.

Are you an emerging spirit
Waking up for the first time?

I enjoy dancing with my heart, out in the world and discovering that I am not alone. Look at the world through the eyes of a dancer, of joy. Do you feel your Spirit waking up? Determine for your own mind and beliefs, are you evolving to be whole with God? As any parent, God witnessing His children loving more and acknowledging His gifts gives the Father the greatest joy.

In Wayne Dyer's book *Pulling Your Own Strings,* he writes, "This is the only life you get, and it is too precious to let others take their advantage of it."

Your life is God's gift to you. How you use this life is your gift to God. Wake up and realize you are the star, it's your show and you are at center stage.

Spiritual Dancer

Selecting dance partners

We are social creatures. We enjoy being around others and learn our communication habits from a variety of sources. We often develop our personal characteristics by how others interact with us. So how do we determine who our dance partners will be?

Community. My first partners were my family. I was surrounded by them most of the time since I was born. My mother spoke to me early in the mornings and dressed me for the day. Those early years were filled with comfort in understanding that someone was there to help me, feed me and nurture me.

In my first remembrance of school was kindergarten where I was in class surrounded by children my own age. Classes were taught by teachers who made us laugh and conducted experiments with science and what looked to me like magic. There were games and toys to play with.

Life is the ultimate dance partner and those with whom you encounter enter and disappear along the way. Each player makes a mark upon your life and contributes some things that are empowering and some things that are not.

It takes years for anyone to develop the interpersonal skills to begin to examine the partner with whom they will choose to dance. Community grows from your perspective of the world. When you begin to realize your dance is unique you find yourself searching for dance companionship that represents a deeper understanding in you. In high school, I started looking for deeper relationships with those who mirrored my way of thinking. Even though I was a popular student, I developed very few close friends. My dance partners were fellow students who had similar interests and tastes.

Not all those who dance with you will last a lifetime. Some relationships last through college, or just for the summer, or a year. Emerson understood friendships when he wrote, "to find one true friend in a lifetime is a masterpiece of nature." That one true friend is yourself.

When you map out the character of yourself a divine relationship begins with you and God. No longer are you

Spiritual Dancer

just a seeker of truth and wisdom but find yourself
dancing with the Infinite while all others watch you
perform.

37. Parenthood from the Heavens

Parents love their children and give them the best of themselves. They fail them if they do not encourage and instruct them on spreading their wings and becoming their own person.

Parents have challenges. They have to compete with the Internet, video games, peer pressures, social media, so raising a family through the ages keeps getting harder. It's so easy to lay blame for all of society's ills on parenting, but the reality of such argument is futile.

Societies as a whole develop the best and worse in all individuals. It is our choice as to what we desire for ourselves. My mother gave us the gift of worship by dressing us up and taking us to church every week. It was her choice to introduce her children to the legacy of worship as she had growing up.

Without such determination, I wouldn't have had the opportunity or the enrichment of knowledge knowing that God was in my life. My mother insisted we join her choir even though a few of my family members were tone challenged and could not sing on key. It didn't matter.

Lessons are given, Wisdom is earned

In Mary Summer Rain's book, *Spirit Song,* she narrates a bio of her journey with a Native American shaman woman known only to the reader as No-Eyes. No-Eyes, so named because the Chippewa shaman woman was blind from birth, created a spiritual journey for Rain.

No-Eyes' paternal guidance helped create a deeper understanding of Spirit in Rain more than just stories or ideas but something along the lines of peering into one's own conscious mind and examining its content.

Lack of understanding gives rise to a void which a great teacher can fill. We do not receive our entire life's understanding from a single source but from many. Parents cannot be held accountable for the child's entire scope of knowledge. They are but one source. We have other teachers everywhere who step up to the plate to instruct and guide us.

When do you become a parent?

We are all parents as soon as we begin instructing people on how to develop skills to enable them. How well we perform these instructions depends largely on our own internal development.

With every new account when I was employed it seemed I played the role of parent. I was training my personnel how to respond to various crises. Since security is graded on how well one takes care of emergency situations, it was the first lesson given to the crew.

I told funny stories, gave examples, quoted verses from my favorite poets. I mentored them, motivated them, conveyed to them on the importance of continuing education for personal growth. I felt a wonderful excitement to see my associates eager to learn and to see them grow.

I filled the parental role of instructing and encouraging my staff to perform. It became my responsibility to equip the staff with the proper tools for success as employees, but I also wanted to see them succeed in life.

Parenting is not left to the biological parents themselves; it is left to the society as a social entity. At every corner of our existence there are teachers and students. At some moments you might find that you are a teacher and other times you are the student. The idea is to absorb great ideas and to be prepared to teach others.

"Human history, with its forms of government, its revolutions, its wars, and in fact the rise and fall of nations, could be written in terms of the rise and fall of ideas implanted in the minds of men."
Herbert Hoover

Spiritual Dancer

We must recognize that ideas produce power. A purpose for training is not just to give directions but to empower the student to reach their greatest potential. Give them motivation to begin a great idea and to have the confidence to complete it. In completion is power and the world can marvel at what mind has created.

38. Nothing Short of Hard Work

In the book, *The Law and The Promise* by Neville Goddard, he states, "Man is free to imagine whatever he desires. This is why, despite all fatalists and misguided prophets of doom, all awakened men know that they are free". Free as the human race to labor as long and as hard as we choose to reach our desires. It is the sweat and hard labor of our own doing that will give us the rewards of ownership of our ideas and our mind.

I believe there are no short cuts. It will not be easy in fact to tame the wild horse we refer to as our mind; it will be the hardest most complicated task you will ever encounter. My life changed my thoughts on how to participate in my own random discoveries. I tried shortcuts which only led to frustration. The problem was never my enthusiasm but my willingness to work hard for results. I had to work harder at discovering myself. I had to limit my outside influences and concentrate on my own brain and tend to my own business.

> *The road to easy street runs*
> *through the sewer*
> Flip Wilson

We might want to believe that dedication to anything worth having is easy. Why most people give up their life's ambitions are because it took a lot of sacrifice and hard work. Do not give in to this misrepresentation of your abilities. You are divine in Spirit, you are brilliant in heart, and you are magnificent in mind.

All of us will find times in our lives when things and plans do not work out the way we had planned. Welcome to the game called life. Life is not static, it keeps moving ahead.

Spiritual Dancer

*The good news is that moment you decided that what
you know is more important than what you
have been taught to believe,
you will have shifted gears in your quest for
abundance. Success comes from within,
not from without.*
Ralph Waldo Emerson

Understanding and appreciating your gifts is a labor of love. It's not something you have to do, but a task you want to do joyfully. The work it requires is a matter of preference. Hard work has the taste of something really dreadful but if it matters then real knowledge begins. The problem with too many pop philosophies or popular cures is all you have to do is to think a little positive thought and then results occur instantaneously; but the real method is the work behind it.

As a piano player and composer, I worked for years to get that perfect carefree melody. I still move my fingers around certain chord progressions for hours to just get a few notes to please my ears. After several days of practicing I might come up with some song that pleases me. However, because of my routine of practicing and creating, some songs are composed overnight or in an evening; I wouldn't sell this as a method to writing songs. It does not always happen this way! It is the practicing that leads to instantly creating material not the other way around.

In all labor there is profit.
Proverbs 14:23

We have made labor a sinful thing. In our teachings we have called labor a burden. But labor is the love of doing, keeping us busy about our day. Labor is the law of consequence. Enjoy the journey of watching how your labor of love influences your growth. There is no secret to labor just begin it, do it, enjoy it. As you prepare for each day, thank the Universal Mind, God, Spirit, The Great I Am, for allowing you to labor this day in loving awareness of your being. Be in the moment of loving the effects of your labor.

Do not compare your growth to someone else. Each plant in your garden grows at its own pace. My father built a construction business based on two important ideas: he was willing to work extremely hard to make up for the lack of knowledge. But he had a very strong will to continue to learn, to grow. With those philosophies, he was extremely successful. Learning to understand labor is the main ingredient in accepting your inner strength.

Discovering a Sense of Power

We work hard at school, work, college, relationships, families, business, but we are a little lazy when it comes to putting the same intense energy into self-awareness. Why do we not show the same diligence for self-discovery?

Why do some people make complex things appear so easy? How does Elton John make piano playing look so effortless? Or Whitney Houston's singing so flawless, or Hemingway's words so easy to read? It was practice, work, commitment to laborious effort to perfect one's talent and abilities.

For example, begin by writing down everything you did today. Keep this notebook for several days. After a few days, review it. How much did you do for yourself? How many books did you take to bed that would better your life? How often did you clear your mind and allow the greater energy of God to enter your life?

You might acknowledge that most of the days are spent in cleaning the house, wrestling with children and rushing them off to school, preparing for the business brief to meet a deadline. What about some time during the day for yourself? Each day when you have a chance for some time, perhaps at lunch, instead you are thinking about what you have do after lunch for your busy day.

Spiritual Dancer

Change right now. Begin each day rewarding yourself by realizing that this moment is a wondrous day which will be filled with the labor of love, no matter what it is. Take that time to dance with The Great I Am. Be willing to make mistakes. Do not beat yourself up. Get up from the ground of despair and begin your labor again. Every day create a method of discovering your genius.

39. Dreaming

Keeping a dream journal is an important exercise in your spiritual dancing. Dreams are open doors to several levels within your mind which communicate vital information. Consider making a practice of keeping a small notebook at your bedside so when you wake up you can record your dreams. It is important not to try to place any significance to your dreams as sometimes they are just ramblings or fantasies but the practice of journaling will allow you to observe how your mind works.

All great mystics and religions give credence to dreams and dream interpretations. In the Bible, God speaks to several prophets in a dream. Joseph, who had been thrown out by his brothers, was able to interpret the dream of the Pharaoh which helped define the country's years of prosperity.

I have been recording my dreams since 1968. A few times I was able to foresee things before they happened. Once I had foreseen an accident I was going to have. Unfortunately, I forgot the dream until I had the accident. The dent in my car was exactly like the one in my dream and that's when I remembered the dream.

Why do dreams have so much importance? In the midst of reality dreams represent something you have little insight. Freud had a great interest in dreams and made several documented studies and interpretations of dreams to understand mental abnormalities. Freud attached several pleasure labels to certain images associated with our dreams and felt he had uncovered a doorway into the unconscious mind. But are dreams really the sign of the unconscious mind working or just the mind having random thoughts?

In his book, *Creativity: The Magic Synthesis,* Silvano Arieti believed dreams are an internal, private occurrence he labeled *endocept (*from the Greek *endo,* inside). His thesis was distinguishing the concept which was expressed by experiences which produce the thought. Arieti's book also makes reference to other writers using endocept as nonverbal, unconscious, or preconscious cognition.

In his book, Arieti reviewed how artists, poets, writers and musicians create their work. His research noted that people who had dreams were not always able to verbalize what they saw or felt in their dreams. He called this process an "Endocept Phenomena". When interviewing the subjects they described these experiences as "diffused" and "abstract". It is more in line with what we did as kids called daydreaming. Freud referred to it as "oceanic" feelings or thoughts in a spark of a moment where we were somewhere else as children and couldn't always explain what we were thinking.

Arieti places some dreams in this category. Mainly, the reason we cannot always remember our dreams is because we might not be able to verbalize your feelings.

In order to value your dreams, begin simply by writing them down. Picasso left a canvas by his bed in his later years so he wouldn't have to get out of bed. Once awake he started immediately to record his ideas on canvas.

Does the mind really turn off as we sleep? Research shows that the mind stays active even while we sleep. We can hear noises around us and the brainwaves drift into a more relaxed stage, but we are aware of the environment around us. However, our dreaming is a method of healing the body and the mind, allowing the body to reboot itself. Research shows that several hormones, such as serotonin, are pumped into the blood stream to revive our mind and repair our body systems.

Dreams are a way of recovery

Medically, we are recovering and repairing in our dream state. In a mystical sense, we are unlocking those hidden thoughts we allow to slip into our unconscious cavity. The act of dreaming gives credence to the idea that certain memories are embedded in our minds that we have yet to deal with and that may be why these are not readily available in our conscious mind. Jotting down thoughts and dreams gives you an opportunity to look back on those thoughts and dreams even though some may be difficult to comprehend.

Dreams are layers of unconscious thoughts. Sometimes I noticed in my own recordings of my dreams that ideas usually unrelated are strung together almost at random within the dream. Do not become discouraged because your dreams make no sense; not all dreams are supposed to.

The mind is constantly recording thoughts, impressions, events, and it stores these away. Can you imagine over a lifetime, the amount of these that exist in our mind? When the mind is relaxed, whether through meditation, daydreaming, or sleeping, it throws out these thoughts. You may not be able to understand nor interpret some of these thoughts. Other thoughts from your dreams, however, may enable you to heal some wounds, solve a problem, or simply enjoy a forgotten, joyful memory.

40. What Type of Dancer Are You?

Welcome the spiritual dance with God. On this dance floor God leads, you follow. If you choose to follow you will never be out of step. The music will always be at the right tempo and the band will always play your favorite songs. In this dance you are the co-creator of your existence on Earth. Is this the type of dancer you want to be?

What choices are you going make? Are you going to choose to be a dancer stuck with the same old song of woe and depression? Do you really want to dance or are you too embarrassed or afraid of what others might say? Maybe you have fallen into despair. Into fear. What type of dancer are you? What type of dancer do you want to be?

My mom had her family sitting at her bedside in the nursing home during her last hours. She was in a deep sleep state but when we talked to her she squeezed our hands. Though dementia took her mind, it did not take her spirit. She knew her family was there surrounding her with love. Her family laughed and shared stories of some of the crazy things we did as kids and how she caught us. We thanked her for her dedication, for her love for us, and her commitment to our education and how much we loved her. And then she took her final breath. These were her gifts to us in her lifetime. She allowed her children to witness her dance with The Great I Am.

What kind of dancer are you going to be? Are you going to lead a life of hopelessness or one of joy-filled? The music is playing. The stage is set. The players in the band have tuned their instruments and are ready to play. The Mighty God reaches out to you for your embrace. Are you ready to dance? Or are you going to sit this one out? The choice is yours.

And so it is.

Spiritual Dancer

Appendix – Resources

There are so many books available on the topics covered in this book. For those who want more in-depth reading, here are some resources that I've compiled for easy reference.

Books

Ahlquist, Diane. *The Complete Idiot's Guide to The Law of Attraction.* Penguin Group, 2008.

Arieti, Silvano. *Creativity: The Magic Synthesis.* Basic Books, 1976.

Cousins, Norman. *Anatomy of an Illness as perceived by the patient: reflections on healing, 1979.*

Covey, Stephen R. *The 7 Habits of Highly Effective People.* Free Press, 1989.

Dyer, Wayne W., Dr. *Pulling Your Own Strings: Dynamic Techniques for Dealing with Other People and Living Your Life as You Choose.* Funk and Wagnalls Co, 1978.

Fombrun, Charles J. *Turning Points: Creating Strategic Change in Corporations.* McGraw Hills Corp, 1992.

Gawain, Shakti. *Living in the Light: Follow Your Inner Guidance to Create a New Life and a New World.* New World Library, Nataraj, 2011.

Gates, Bill. *The Road Ahead.* Viking Books, 1995.

Goddard, Neville. *The Law and The Promise.* DeVorss and Co, 1984.

Goleman, Daniel. *Emotional Intelligence.* Bantam Books, 1995.

Gray, John. *Men are from Mars, Women are from Venus.* Harper Collins, 1992.

Holmes, Earnest. *The Science of Mind.* Tarcher Putnam, 1926.

James, William. *Pragmatism and Other Writings.* Penguin Books, 2000.

Maltz, Maxwell, Dr. *Psycho-Cybernetics, A New Way to Get More Living Out of Life.* Wilshire Books Co, 1967.

McCullough, David. *John Adams.* Simon & Schuster, 2002.

Nash, Ogden. *Marriage Lines.* Little Hampton Book Service Ltd, 1964.

Ornstein, Robert, and Sobel, David. *The Healing Brain: Breakthrough Discoveries About How the Brain Keeps Us Healthy.* Simon & Schuster, 1987.

Rain, Mary Summer. *Spirit Song: The Introduction of No-Eyes.* Hampton Roads Publishing, 1993.

Rama, Swami. *Living with the Himalayan Masters.* Himalayan Institute Press, 2007.

Rinpocke, Akong Tulku. *Taming the Tiger.* Rider, 1994.

Ruiz, Don Miguel. *The Four Agreements.* Amber-Allen Publishing, 1997.

Schucman, Helen. *The Course in Miracles.* Foundation for Inner Peace, 1972.

Smith, O. C., and Shaw, James. *Little Green Apples: God Really Did Make Them!* Devorss and Co, 2003.

About the Author

Fred has been writing for over 40 years. He is married to his wife, Karen, for nearly 20 years. They currently live primarily in Republic of Panama, Florida, and California.

Fred's poetry has been published in several magazines including: *Spiritual Winds, Pasadena Weekly, Red Owl Magazine, and Black Romance Magazine.*

He has self-published a book of poetry called, *Notes from a Whimsical Observer.* It is in its second printing.

His essays have appeared in over 30 newspapers including: *The Black Achiever, The Pasadena Star News, The Los Angeles Times.* On-line magazines including the *securityprofessionalsite.com* have also published his essays.

His screenplay, "Courage Knows No Bounds", won him a finalist position in Los Angeles Black Film Festival, *The Writer's Digest* and The Austin Film Festival 2006.

Fred was a network contributor to *Yahoo.com* as well as had over 50 articles, poetry, and cartoons published.

Fred has written short films featured on YouTube under *fleetwriter*: a series of "Barology" episodes, and "How to Interview a Vampire".

Fred's latest publications are: *Investing @ The Speed of Success* and his first suspense novel *Dark Cloaks and Nightmares* on Amazon.